DISCARD

101 TV SHOWS

TO SEE BEFORE YOU GROW UP

BE YOUR OWN TV CRITIC—
THE MUST-SEE TV LIST FOR KIDS

Since its invention, television has entertained families around the world! The best shows are creative, innovative, and memorable. There are characters that steal your heart, ideas that inspire, and exciting fantasy worlds. This book is filled with 101 of the most popular TV shows for families, children, and couch potatoes of all ages. Use it as your own personal TV Guide, and learn cool trivia and behind-the-scenes details to look out for as you watch each show. Then check the show off your list after you've seen it. Each profile calls out essential details like who created the show, how many seasons were produced, and the ages that will enjoy the show. You'll also pick up other fun facts you can use to impress your friends. From classic educational shows to laugh-out-loud sitcoms, animated adventures, puppet musicals, and more, you'll find plenty of shows here to create your own TV bucket list. So grab some popcorn, claim your spot on the couch, and let the fun begin!

Quarto is the authority on a wide range of topics. Quarto educates, entertains, and enriches the lives of our readers—enthusiasts and lovers of hands-on living. www.quartoknows.com

© 2017 Quarto Publishing Group USA Inc.
Published by Walter Foster Jr.,
an imprint of Quarto Publishing Group USA Inc.
All rights reserved. Walter Foster Jr. is trademarked.

Written by Samantha Chagollan and Erika Milvy
Illustrated by Natasha Hellegouarch

6 Orchard Road, Suite 100
Lake Forest, CA 92630
quartoknows.com
Visit our blogs at quartoknows.com

Printed in China
1 3 5 7 9 10 8 6 4 2

MIX
Paper from responsible sources
FSC® C101537

101 TV SHOWS

TO SEE BEFORE YOU GROW UP

After you watch each show, join the fun by using the blanks below each profile to record your own rating.

The suggested age ranges in this book are taken from Common Sense Media or reflect the authors' best recommendations. Be sure to talk with your parents before watching a new show.

The best way to watch TV is with the people you love!

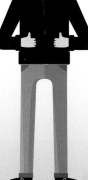

WRITTEN BY SAMANTHA CHAGOLLAN AND ERIKA MILVY
ILLUSTRATED BY NATASHA HELLEGOUARCH

TABLE OF CONTENTS

The shows in this book are divided by genre and listed in random order, so you can start watching wherever you like. Enjoy!

1

SESAME STREET

GENRE:
Educational

AGE:
2+

SEASONS:
47 and counting

MADE BY:
Joan Ganz
Cooney

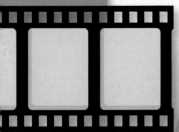

"Sally, you've never seen a street like
Sesame Street. Everything happens
here. You're gonna love it!"
— The first line in the first episode,
November, 1969

Sesame Street is TV at its finest, funniest, and furriest. Launched in 1969 and still adored today, *Sesame Street* is a groundbreaking show set on a diverse city block where puppets and humans of all ages mingle and learn from one another. The lessons, filled with humor and friendship, aim to help viewers learn to read, count, and understand feelings, relationships, and the world around them. Sidewalk action is interspersed with short, live-action films; animation; and music, plus witty parodies and A-list guest stars that parents love.

The cast includes some adult actors and plenty of kids, but it's Jim Henson's amazing Muppets that steal the show and viewers' hearts. Bert and Ernie, the odd couple of Muppets, show that you can be best friends with someone who is very different from you. Oscar the Grouch lets viewers know it's okay to be cranky sometimes. And Cookie Monster's sugar cravings, Grover's enthusiasm, and Big Bird's curiosity are all things we can relate to.

"Can you tell me how to get, how to get to Sesame Street?" This familiar line from the theme song has comforted generations of kids. The show initially aired on public television and is now available on HBO, so classic songs like Oscar's "I Love Trash," Cookie Monster's "C is for Cookie," and Ernie's "Rubber Ducky," can be sung by a new generation!

STARRING:
Jim Henson's Muppets, and Puppeteers and voice actors like Frank Oz

NETWORK:
PBS, HBO

SPIN-OFFS

Elmo's World
Play with Me Sesame
Journey to Ernie
Bert and Ernie's Great Adventures
Abby's Flying Fairy School
Elmo the Musical

DID YOU KNOW?

The pink, pigtailed puppet Abby Cadabby speaks her own language. She calls it Dragonfly.

Saw it! ☐ Rating: ☆☆☆☆☆

Date: ___/___/_____ With: _____

Notes: _____

_____

2

BILL NYE THE SCIENCE GUY

GENRE:
Educational

AGE:
7+

SEASONS:
5

STARRING:
Bill Nye

With his peppy bow ties and impressively broad areas of expertise, Bill Nye is one of the coolest scientists in our stratosphere. In this classic show, Nye plays the role of the mad scientist and shares his enthusiasm for biology, physics, chemistry, and the natural world with viewers. A variety of creative experiments and upbeat segments make it clear why Nye finds science so fascinating.

The show covers gravity, dinosaurs, biodiversity, sound, the moon, digestion, cells, eyeballs, electricity, and so much more. In one regular feature, "Way Cool Scientist," Nye talks to an expert in the field. "Nifty Home Experiments" show viewers how to "try this at home." "Soundtrack of Science" segments include music videos like "Evolution" sung to the tune of "Revolution" by The Beatles. Vintage film footage, sketches, fake commercials, and kid input also keep the show lively.

Nye has a knack for explaining complex ideas in memorable ways. In one episode, he runs around a soccer field to show how big the solar system is, even jumping in his car and driving to where Pluto would be. Many teachers use Bill Nye segments to introduce science topics to their classes, and young scientists often say it was Bill Nye that made them fans of science.

DID YOU KNOW?
Carl Sagan was Nye's teacher. Nye studied mechanical engineering at Cornell University and took classes with the famous astronomer.

Saw it! ☐ Rating: ☆☆☆☆☆
Date: ___/___/_____ With: _____
Notes: _____
_____

PEPPA PIG

Snort along with Peppa and the Pig family in this delightfully silly series where everyone likes to play games and have fun together. Peppa is a cheeky British piggy who plays hide-and-seek with her little brother George Pig. Together they have adventures with her friends Suzy Sheep, Danny Dog, Emily Elephant, Candy Cat, and Rebecca Rabbit. They jump in muddy puddles, go on treasure hunts, fly kites, and take bicycle rides. Peppa also loves to blow raspberries, burp, and of course, snort with her family.

GENRE:
Educational

AGE:
3+

Peppa Pig first aired in 2004, and is still going strong. Each five-minute episode is about friendship, family, laughter, and imagination. Peppa is quite popular—her show is watched and loved in more than 180 countries around the world. The official website is filled with games and print-and-color pages, and includes a separate site for grown-ups with lessons, apps, and activities. Peppa's adventures have even inspired a theme park, Peppa Pig World, in Hampshire, England, where a million visitors each year get to see Peppa's world up close. Visitors can jump in muddy puddles, take a ride on Miss Rabbit's helicopter, and visit Peppa's house. Whether you're palling around with Peppa in Pig World or watching her show, you can be assured it will be lots of snorty fun!

SEASONS:
6 and counting

STARRING:
Lily Snowden-Fine,
John Sparkes,
Alice May,
Morwenna Banks,
Richard Ridings,
and
Oliver May

DID YOU KNOW?

Several different actors voice Peppa as she gets older throughout the series.

Saw it! ☐ Rating: ☆☆☆☆☆
Date: ___ / ___ / _____ With: _____
Notes: _____
_____

4

READING RAINBOW

GENRE:
Educational

AGE:
4+

SEASONS:
21

STARRING:
LeVar Burton

When this show first aired in 1983, some skeptics doubted whether TV was the best forum for encouraging reading. But 155 episodes and 26 Emmys later, *Reading Rainbow* proved that TV and reading do mix.

Produced and hosted by LeVar Burton, the show features interviews with a wide variety of authors, such as Maya Angelou and Pete Seeger. Celebs such as Whoopi Goldberg, Susan Sarandon, Martin Short, Helen Mirren, James Earl Jones, and Run DMC narrate each episode and sometimes make guest appearances. There are field trips and mini documentaries on topics such as dinosaurs, deserts, and recycling. In other segments, kids talk about their favorite books.

Each episode focuses on a theme. In one episode about emotions, LeVar talks about why he feels bad, a film about Koko the Gorilla, who was given a kitten when she felt sad, is shown, and an animated segment has kids reading poems about their feelings.

This long-running multicultural celebration of books features a wide variety of genres, cultures, and formats—making it a true reading rainbow!

DID YOU KNOW?

When the show went off the air, LeVar Burton bought the rights, hoping he could someday launch the series again. While the show hasn't returned to TV, Burton raised over $5 million to create the popular Reading Rainbow Skybrary app, which is filled with interactive books and videos.

Saw it! ☐ Rating: ☆☆☆☆☆
Date: ___/___/_____ With: _____
Notes: _____
_____

MISTER ROGERS' NEIGHBORHOOD

A landmark show, *Mister Rogers' Neighborhood* is a play date with Fred Rogers, a sweet-as-can-be neighbor who talks in the gentlest way. Viewers regularly feel like Mr. Rogers is coming home from work to spend some time with them. He comes through his door and speaks directly to the camera as he changes into his sneakers and cardigan sweater.

Mister Rogers' Neighborhood isn't hip, zany, or loud. It's not action packed or filled with quick cuts, stimulating motion, or flashing colors. Rather, it is an engaging show filled with honest communication and imagination. Rogers brings viewers along on field trips, demonstrates crafts or experiments, and visits with neighbors. One favorite feature is "The Neighborhood of Make-Believe," where viewers watch a toy trolley enter a kingdom populated by puppet characters like Cornflake S. Pecially and Daniel Striped Tiger. Providing a consistent routine for viewers by singing "Won't You Be My Neighbor?" at the beginning of each episode and "It's Such a Good Feeling" at the end, this is as cozy as TV gets!

GENRE:
Educational

AGE:
4+

SEASONS:
31

STARRING:
Fred Rogers

DID YOU KNOW?

Koko, a famous gorilla that communicates with scientists using American Sign Language, loves watching *Mister Rogers' Neighborhood* in her spare time. When Rogers visited Koko on his show, she knew exactly who he was and took his shoes off, just like he does at the beginning of each episode!

Saw it! ☐ Rating: ☆☆☆☆☆

Date: ___ / ___ / _____ With: _____

Notes: _____

_____

6

THE ELECTRIC COMPANY

GENRE:
Educational

AGE:
5+

SEASONS:
6

STARRING:
Morgan Freeman,
Judy Graubart,
Skip Hinnant,
Rita Moreno, and
Jim Boyd

From the Children's Television Workshop comes a *Sesame Street* for the 1970s elementary-school set. Making use of sketch comedy, cartoons, and songs, the show teaches phonics, spelling, and grammar, while entertaining viewers long after they master these skills.

The show features many memorable characters. There's Fargo North, Decoder, a detective who has the ability to decode messages by making sentences out of jumbled words. Comedian Joan Rivers is part of the cast, as is Morgan Freeman, who plays Easy Reader, a smooth soul man who loves reading. Rita Moreno began her career on the show, and her loud holler, "Hey, you guys!" became the show's tagline. Other regular characters include Vincent the Vegetable Vampire, Lorelei the Chicken, and Pandora the Brat. The show even features guest stars such as Oscar the Grouch and Big Bird.

Each show is broken into mini episodes. Live-action skits parody popular soap operas, cooking shows, and monster movies. Whatever segment you love best, you'll finish every episode of *The Electric Company* thinking, "*Power on!*"

DID YOU KNOW?

The Electric Company included a regular segment called "Spidey Super Stories," where Spider-Man catches criminals and speaks through word balloons.

Saw it! ☐ Rating: ☆☆☆☆☆
Date: ___/ ___/ _____ With: _____
Notes: _____
_____

WHERE IN THE WORLD IS CARMEN SANDIEGO?

7

A game show that makes geography fun for everyone, *Where in the World Is Carmen Sandiego?* is an international sensation based on a series of computer games. Contestants, called "gumshoes," are hired by the Acme Crime Detective Agency to track down one of Carmen Sandiego's henchmen.

In each episode, Carmen Sandiego, a "sticky-fingered filcher," and her gang of crooks circle the globe while host Greg Lee challenges three gumshoes to follow the clues and find the thieves. The skits, quizzes, and games are non-stop fun, and the stakes are high for each group of gumshoes—they are competing for a grand prize trip to anywhere in North America.

The show was the first game show to air on PBS, and also the second-longest-running game show for kids in TV history (beaten only by *Double Dare*). It received a Peabody award, several Emmys, and was ranked in the Top 50 Greatest Game Shows of All Time by *TV Guide*. The National Academy of Recording Arts and Sciences also says the show's theme song, written by Sean Altman and David Yazbek, is one of the most recognized TV theme songs in history.

GENRE:
Educational

AGE:
7+

SEASONS:
5

STARRING:
Greg Lee and
Rita Moreno

DID YOU KNOW?

In the early 1990s, borders were changing rapidly, so many episodes ended with a disclaimer saying "all geographic information was accurate as of the date this program was recorded."

Saw it! ☐ Rating: ☆☆☆☆☆
Date: ___ / ___ / _____ With: _____
Notes: _____
_____

8

SCHOOLHOUSE ROCK

GENRE:
Educational

AGE:
5+

SEASONS:
7

MADE BY:
David McCall
and Tom Yohe

"I'm just a bill. Yes, I'm only a bill.
And I'm sitting here on Capitol Hill.
Well, it's a long, long journey to the capital city."
—From the lyrics to "I'm Just a Bill"

This iconic series was a stroke of educational programming genius. Airing between cartoons on Saturday mornings, the animated shorts feature songs that are so catchy, adults still sing them today. The songs teach concepts by pairing them with memorable characters and catchy lyrics. In "I'm Just a Bill," simple lessons explain how a bill becomes a law.

The program was created by David McCall, an ad man who noticed his son could remember all the lyrics to Beatles' songs but not his multiplication tables. Viewers can watch everything from "My Hero Zero" to "Naughty Number Nine" to learn their multiplication tables. *Grammar Rock* explains word usage and answers questions with songs like "Unpack Your Adjectives," "Lolly, Lolly, Lolly, Get Your Adverbs Here," and "A Noun Is A Person, Place Or Thing." With this show, whatever topic you're interested in, you'll find learning rocks!

STARRING:
Jack Sheldon,
Darrell Stern,
and
Sue Manchester

SPIN-OFFS

America Rock
Multiplication Rock
Grammar Rock
Science Rock
Money Rock
Scooter Computer and Mr. Chips

DID YOU KNOW?

To coincide with the United States bicentennial in 1976, *Schoolhouse Rock* introduced *America Rock,* with segments on government and American history.

NETWORK:
ABC, Disney

Saw it! ☐   Rating: ☆☆☆☆☆
Date: ___/___/_____   With: _____
Notes: _____
_____

9

MYTHBUSTERS

GENRE:
Educational

AGE:
9+

SEASONS:
14

MADE BY:
Peter Rees

*"I don't think our death ray is working.
I'm standing right in it and I'm not dead yet."*
—Jamie Hyneman

MythBusters is a science show that takes learning out of the lab and into more dramatic settings. Two Hollywood special-effects experts, Jamie Hyneman and Adam Savage, conduct experiments to confirm or debunk urban legends. They use the scientific method, trial and error, and astute problem-solving skills to determine if myths and rumors are factually sound. Each episode results with a conclusion that labels a myth "busted," "plausible," or "confirmed." The humorous duo answers pressing questions: *Can tooth fillings receive radio waves? Can being covered with gold paint actually be deadly? Do frozen chickens cause more damage than thawed chickens when shot at a plane's windshield?*

The action-packed, bizarre experiments are always highly entertaining; there are car crashes, bangs, blasts, and pyrotechnics. Along the way, viewers learn a lot about science, exploring questions like: *exactly how many bacteria do reside on a toothbrush?* The hosts also tackle far-fetched plots from movies (*Can a person be really sucked down by killer quicksand?* Watch to find out!), and even construct the weirdest things. In one episode, Adam and Jamie are left on a deserted island with nothing but a pile of duct tape. They make a series of nifty devices, including a duct-tape canoe to get them home. Join the *MythBusters* as they put these wacky myths to the test!

STARRING:
Jamie Hyneman
and
Adam Savage

NETWORK:
Discovery
Channel

SPIN-OFFS
Head Rush
Search for the Next MythBusters

DID YOU KNOW?
The hosts have worked on special effects for a wide variety of popular movies, including *The Matrix* and *Star Wars* series.

Saw it! ☐   Rating: ☆☆☆☆☆
Date: ___ / ___ / _____ With: _____
Notes: _____
_____

SHOW NO.

10 THE MUPPET SHOW

GENRE:
Puppets

AGE:
4+

SEASONS:
5

MADE BY:
Jim Henson

Waldorf: These seats are awful.
Statler: Why? Can't you see anything?
Waldorf: That's the problem. I can see everything.

18

Preschoolers aren't the only people who adore Kermit and the fuzzy puppets from *Sesame Street. The Muppet Show* is a variety show in which the puppets do more than sing and dance. They play "real" actors who have off-stage lives and backstage crises. Kermit the Frog, always the most grown-up Muppet, is the producer who oversees the drama-filled cast, including Miss Piggy, a diva with lots of demands. The other Muppets include Fozzie Bear, who frequently performs really bad stand-up; Gonzo the Great, who does stunts; Rowlf the Dog; Scooter; Animal; and the house rock band, Dr. Teeth and The Electric Mayhem. The show features favorite sketches like "Muppet Melodrama," in which Miss Piggy is often in danger; "Pigs in Space," a *Star Trek* spoof; "Muppet Labs," which features Dr. Bunsen Honeydew's latest inventions (with frequent malfunctions); and "Muppet News Flash," an absurd news program.

Many of these skits and parodies are designed to appeal to viewers of all ages. Because of the vaudeville format, there's a great variety of acts, and the breezy pace keeps viewers' attention. Each episode features A-list human guest stars such as Elton John, Gene Kelley, Steve Martin, Harry Bellafonte, Roy Rodgers, and Rudolf Nureyev. The Muppets went on to star in a wildly entertaining collection of popular movies, and in 2015, a new take on the old series began airing on TV.

STARRING:
Puppeteers:
Jim Henson,
Frank Oz, and
Richard Hunt

NETWORK:
ITV

SPIN-OFFS

Muppet Babies
The Great Muppet Caper
The Muppets Take Manhattan
The Jim Henson Hour
Muppet Treasure Island
The Muppet Christmas Carol
Muppets from Space

DID YOU KNOW?
Kermit is the only Muppet character to appear on both *Sesame Street* and *The Muppet Show*.

Saw it! ☐ Rating: ☆☆☆☆☆
Date: ___ / ___ / _____ With: _____
Notes: _____
_____

19

11

FRAGGLE ROCK

GENRE:
Puppets

AGE:
6+

SEASONS:
5

MADE BY:
Jim Henson

Mokey Fraggle: It was rapturous!
Red Fraggle: Is rapturous the same as boring?
Wembley Fraggle: I don't think so.

Those who are hankering for more Muppets can let the music play (clap, clap)! *Fraggle Rock* introduces Fraggles, Doozers, and Gorgs, all new furry species created by Jim Henson. These cave-dwelling creatures inhabit a rock formation behind a hole in a garage that belongs to an eccentric inventor named Doc. The Fraggles call Doc's workshop "outer space," and try to avoid the "silly creatures," or humans, that live there. The Fraggles, Doozers, and Gorgs live in a complex society. Most Fraggles play a lot and work a little, while the tiny Doozers work a lot and play a little. Outside of Fraggle Rock, a family of giant Gorg trolls stomp carelessly, as they attempt to rule the universe, despite being simple farmers.

STARRING:
Gerard Parkes, Karen Prell, and Kathryn Mullen

It's a loopy mix of characters, but they all depend on each other. Every episode uses a light touch to present themes of connection, responsibility, and teamwork. Story lines address identity, social conflict, prejudice, and the environment, but *Fraggle Rock* is also a silly musical with loads of energy and humor for both adults and kids. This show is a joy to watch—whether you're dancing your cares away down at Fraggle Rock or watching in your living room.

NETWORK:
CBC, HBO

SPIN-OFFS

Fraggle Rock: The Animated Series
Jim Henson's Doozers

DID YOU KNOW?

The Fraggles were originally known as Woozles.
Jim Henson changed the name to avoid confusion with the
woozles in A.A. Milne's Winnie the Pooh stories.

Saw it! ☐   Rating: ☆☆☆☆☆
Date: ___/___/_____ With: _____
Notes: _____
_____

12

THE BRADY BUNCH

GENRE:
Sitcom

AGE:
7+

SEASONS:
5

MADE BY:
Sherwood
Schwartz

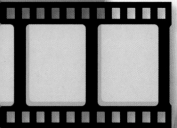

*"All day long at school I hear how great
Marcia is at this or how wonderful Marcia
did that! Marcia, Marcia, Marcia!"*
—Jan Brady

It's oh-so-1970s and more than a little corny, but this story of a lovely lady, a handsome fellow, and their blended family is a pioneering sitcom. Rather than presenting divorce and stepparents as something to be feared, the show features a family that makes building new relationships seem fun and easy. *The Brady Bunch*, which ran from 1969–1974, tells the story of a father with three sons who marries a mother of three girls. Robert Reed played Mike Brady, a successful architect in Southern California, and Florence Henderson played Carol Brady. She runs their large suburban home with the help of their wise-cracking, live-in housekeeper, Alice Nelson. The kids include Greg, the eldest; Peter, the mischievous one; and Bobby, the annoying little brother. There's also Marcia, who's super popular; Jan, who's jealous of her popular sister; and Cindy, the baby of the family.

During the show's five seasons, the kids' ages ranged from 7–18 years old. By including boys and girls of all ages, the show appeals to a wide audience and addresses almost any issue you can think of, from sibling rivalry, popularity, and independence to honesty and competition. And they also encounter some not-so-typical comic situations—like finding out that the only reason a talent agency wants to make you into a rock star is because you fit inside an ornate gold matador suit! Whatever episode you watch, this show is sure to give you lots of groovy giggles!

STARRING:
Robert Reed,
Florence Henderson,
Ann B. Davis,
Barry Williams,
Maureen McCormick,
Christopher Knight,
Eve Plumb,
Mike Lookinland,
and
Susan Olsen

NETWORK:
ABC

SPIN-OFFS

The Brady Kids
The Brady Bunch Variety Hour
The Brady Girls Get Married
A Very Brady Christmas
The Bradys

DID YOU KNOW?

While there was often a camera in the Brady bathroom, the network censors never allowed the toilet to be shown.

Saw it! ☐ Rating: ☆☆☆☆☆
Date: ___/___/_____ With: _____
Notes: _____
_____

13

BOY MEETS WORLD

GENRE:
Sitcom

AGE:
10+

SEASONS:
7

STARRING:
Ben Savage,
Rider Strong,
Danielle Fishel,
and
William Daniels

Growing up is never easy, but having true friends makes it easier. This show follows average kid and all-around good guy Cory Matthews from middle school through college. With his best friend, Shawn Hunter, by his side, Cory navigates friendships, school, and crushes. Free spirit Topanga Lawrence is Cory's super smart classmate, but could she be so much more?

Over seven seasons, the friends tackle being grounded, first kisses, bullying, and of course…prom. Even though things may not always go Cory's way, the relationships he depends on help him—and the viewers—learn valuable and relatable life lessons.

While the show wasn't raved about by critics, and never soared in the ratings, a generation of teens grew up devoted to Cory and his friends, and laughed and cried with them all the way to the series finale in 2000.

SPIN-OFFS
Girl Meets World

DID YOU KNOW?
Much of the show was filmed at John Marshall High School, where movies including *Pretty in Pink, Grease, Transformers*, and *Raiders of the Lost Ark* were filmed.

Saw it! ☐ Rating: ☆☆☆☆☆
Date: ___/___/_____ With: _____
Notes: _____
_____

GOOD TIMES

Even though the Evans family is poor and goes through plenty of hardships, they always manage to find the good times. Living in the projects of Chicago, James and Florida Evans do everything they can to make a good life for their three children, J.J., Michael, and Thelma. Michael is the scholarly one in the family—he learns all he can about African-American history, and later gets involved in politics. J.J. is the artistic one—he hopes to be an artist someday. Thelma is the voice of reason.

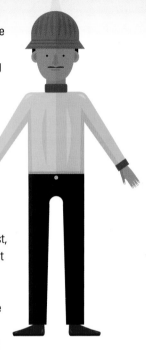

In the mid 1970s, *Good Times* was one of the first sitcoms to feature an African-American cast, providing a glimpse into the American family that audiences hadn't seen before. The issues the Evans struggle with, such as finding work and stretching every dollar to make ends meet, were familiar to many families at the time. Audiences could relate to the show—and laugh along with it too.

GENRE:
Sitcom

AGE:
10+

SEASONS:
6

STARRING:
Esther Rolle,
John Amos,
Jimmie Walker,
Ralph Carter,
BernNadette
Stanis, and
Ja'net DuBois

DID YOU KNOW?
As J.J., Jimmie Walker made his catchphrase, "DY-NO-MITE," a true pop-culture phenomenon!

Saw it! ☐ Rating: ☆☆☆☆☆
Date: ___/___/_____ With: _____
Notes: _____
_____

15

THE FRESH PRINCE OF BEL-AIR

GENRE:
Sitcom

AGE:
11+

SEASONS:
6

MADE BY:
Andy Borowitz
and Susan
Borowitz

"Now this is a story all about how my life got flipped, turned upside down, And I'd like to take a minute, just sit right there, I'll tell you how I became the Prince of a town called Bel-Air..."
—From the classic theme song rapped by Will Smith

Will Smith stars in this fish-out-of-water series, playing a fictionalized version of himself as a teenager sent to live with his wealthy aunt and uncle and their three kids in Bel-Air, California. The new digs are meant to help Will get a better education and stay out of trouble, but the family ends up learning a thing or two about life from Will too.

The Fresh Prince provides much needed positive portrayals of African-American family life. Uncle Phil is a gruff-but-caring lawyer with experience fighting for civil-rights and lots of real-world lessons to share, while Aunt Viv is a career-minded mother and doctor. Carlton, their conservative, preppy son, couldn't be more different than Will. Ashley, the youngest daughter, connects more with the newest member of the family; in one episode, Will encourages her to quit violin and take up the drums after she reveals she doesn't enjoy playing it. Older sister Hilary is a shallow valley girl. The sarcastic butler, Geoffrey, and Will's friend, Jazz, add humor. The series also features a stellar list of guest stars including Whoopi Goldberg, Chris Rock, Dr. Dre, Kareem Abdul-Jabbar, BB King, Isaac Hayes, Queen Latifah, Oprah Winfrey, and many more.

This beloved show combines classic sitcom jokes with serious topics like racial profiling, robbery, and Will's relationship with his dad. Throughout the series, Smith's comedic timing and charisma shine. If you like watching him flash his famous movie-star smile, you'll love watching his career get started on the small screen.

STARRING:
Will Smith,
James Avery,
Janet Hubert,
Alfonso Ribeiro,
Karyn Parsons,
Tatyana Ali,
Joseph Marcell,
and
Daphne Reid

NETWORK:
NBC

DID YOU KNOW?
In 1994, President Donald Trump guest starred as himself. He was interested in buying the Banks' estate, but they decided not to sell.

Saw it! ☐ Rating: ☆☆☆☆☆

Date: ___/___/_____ With: _____

Notes: _____

_____

16

THE WONDER YEARS

GENRE:
Sitcom

AGE:
12+

SEASONS:
6

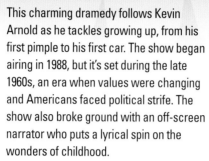

STARRING:
Fred Savage,
Dan Lauria,
Alley Mills,
Olivia d'Abo,
Jason Hervey,
Danica McKellar,
Josh Saviano,
and
Daniel Stern

This charming dramedy follows Kevin Arnold as he tackles growing up, from his first pimple to his first car. The show began airing in 1988, but it's set during the late 1960s, an era when values were changing and Americans faced political strife. The show also broke ground with an off-screen narrator who puts a lyrical spin on the wonders of childhood.

Fred Savage gives an impressive, authentic, often touching performance as Kevin, a sweet, slightly twerpy kid. Winnie Cooper, who goes from friend to girlfriend and back a few times during the span of the series, lives next door. Kevin's obnoxious older brother, Wayne, takes pleasure in tormenting Kevin and his nerdy best friend Paul. Sister Karen is a hippie who butts heads with their gruff father, a Korean War veteran. Mom Norma softens his edges.

While some episodes share plot points with other shows (school dances, dates, sports teams, math tests, cool kids, ethical dilemmas), *The Wonder Years* approaches these issues with nuanced humor, a thoughtful perspective, and high-quality storytelling.

DID YOU KNOW?

Danica McKellar, the actress who played Winnie, wrote a series of books to encourage girls to study math. *Math Doesn't Suck: How to Survive Middle School Math Without Losing Your Mind or Breaking a Nail* is the first title in the series.

Saw it! ☐ Rating: ☆☆☆☆☆

Date: ___ / ___ / _____ With: _____

Notes: _____

_____

BEWITCHED

Darrin Stephens thinks he's marrying an average girl—until his wife Samantha tells him on their honeymoon that she has a little secret…she's a witch! She promises Darrin she won't use her magical powers at home, but as their life together begins, Samantha finds it impossible to refrain from casting a few spells to help her family.

Their home on Morning Glory Circle in Westport, Connecticut is the home of many magical shenanigans. Samantha's mother, Endora, is also a witch and not particularly fond of her mortal son-in-law. Nosy neighbor Gladys Kravitz is always suspicious of Samantha, but she can never quite catch her crafting a spell. Darrin's boss Larry Tate is a frequent visitor, along with Samantha's identical cousin, Serena (also played by Elizabeth Montgomery). Most episodes feature Samantha casting a spell that somehow goes wrong. But she and Darrin are always able to solve the problem together, proving that love is a special kind of magic!

GENRE:
Sitcom

AGE:
7+

SEASONS:
8

STARRING:
Elizabeth Montgomery, Dick York, Dick Sargent, and Agnes Moorhead

DID YOU KNOW?

The opening credits were created by the famous animation team Hanna-Barbera, who developed *The Flintstones*, *The Jetsons*, *Scooby-Doo*, and *The Smurfs*!

Saw it! ☐   Rating: ☆☆☆☆☆
Date: ___ / ___ / _____ With: _____
Notes: _____
_____

18

GILLIGAN'S ISLAND

GENRE:
Sitcom

AGE:
7+

SEASONS:
3

STARRING:
Bob Denver,
Alan Hale, Jr.,
Jim Backus,
Natalie Schafer,
Tina Louise,
Russell Johnson,
and
Dawn Wells

Originally airing in the mid 1960s, *Gilligan's Island* is a light-hearted, goofy comedy about castaways marooned on a deserted island. A skipper and his first mate, Gilligan, take five passengers sight seeing. But a tropical storm ruins what is meant to be "a three-hour tour," and the crew and the passengers must band together to survive.

The castaways send signals to passing boats and planes. They even make a raft. But invariably there's a snag, and it's usually due to one of Gilligan's bumbling blunders. When the survivors include everyone from a professor to a movie star, tensions can rise. But the crew and passengers work together to craft the comforts of home using bamboo, coconuts, and other island materials. With snazzy thatched-roof huts, cozy hammock beds, tropical drinks, a radio built from coconuts, and even a pedal-powered car, viewers can't help but think surviving on this island looks less like a shipwreck and more like a vacation!

SPIN-OFFS
The New Adventures of Gilligan

DID YOU KNOW?
Actor Alan Hale went to great lengths to audition for the role of the skipper. To get there he rode horseback, hitchhiked, took an airplane, and made the last leg of the trip in a taxi!

Saw it! ☐   Rating: ☆☆☆☆☆
Date: ___/___/_____ With: _____
Notes: _____
_____

DIFF'RENT STROKES

Millionaire widower Phillip Drummond promises his housekeeper he will take care of her sons, no matter what. So when she passes away, he adopts 8-year-old Arnold and 12-year-old Willis. Moving into the 30th floor penthouse with their new guardian and new sister, 13-year-old Kimberly, is a big change for Arnold and Willis, but they come to love their new lifestyle. Calling them his sons and treating them like his own children, Mr. Drummond—along with his housekeeper Mrs. Garrett—helps Arnold and Willis learn some important lessons.

  As the smart and lovable Arnold, Gary Coleman is the star of the show. He was 10 years old when the show started filming in 1978; Gary had caught producers' attention in a number of commercials, and the show was created with him in mind.

  A popular show when it debuted, *Diff'rent Strokes* was one of the first shows to feature an interracial family, and the sitcom became known for episodes that tackled dramatic topics, such as racism and kidnapping. Through it all, laughter and love keep this unique family strong, no matter what differences they have to overcome.

SPIN-OFFS
The Facts of Life

GENRE:
Sitcom

AGE:
10+

SEASONS:
8

DID YOU KNOW?
Future superstar Janet Jackson appears as Willis's girlfriend Charlene Duprey in several seasons of the show. Her hit single "Control" debuted while the show was still airing.

STARRING:
Gary Coleman,
Todd Bridges,
Conrad Bain,
and
Dana Plato

Saw it! ☐ Rating: ☆☆☆☆☆
Date: ___ / ___ / _____ With: _____
Notes: _____
_____

20

ALL IN THE FAMILY

GENRE:
Sitcom

AGE:
12+

SEASONS:
9

STARRING:
Carroll
O'Connor,
Jean Stapleton,
Rob Reiner, and
Sally Struthers

All in The Family revolves around a typical working class family from the 1970s. In each episode, Archie Bunker's outspoken bigotry clashes with his son-in-law, Mike Stivic's, liberal views. Archie's wife, Edith, can be a little dense—but she is also the moral and kind voice in the family. Gloria, Mike's wife and Archie and Edith's daughter, acts as the peacemaker.

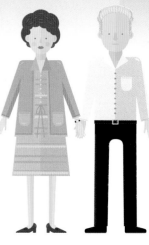

Widely considered to be one of the most groundbreaking shows ever aired, *All in The Family* brought conversations about the current affairs of the 1970s into viewers' living rooms. Debates about politics, social change, race relations, and the changing roles of men and women are only some of the hot-button topics that producer Norman Lear served up at the Bunker family table.

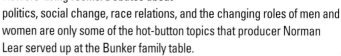

All in the Family still stands as a prime-time example of how TV can entertain and educate all at the same time.

SPIN-OFFS

Archie Bunker's Place
Maude
The Jeffersons

DID YOU KNOW?
Producer Norman Lear said his father inspired many of Archie's best insults. "Meathead," "Dingbat," and "Stifle" were all things Lear heard his father say.

Saw it! ☐ Rating: ☆☆☆☆☆
Date: ___/___/_____ With: _____
Notes: _____
_____

THE GOLDBERGS

Follow 11-year-old Adam Goldberg as he documents his crazy childhood with a totally rad video camera. Set in "1980-something" in suburban Pittsburgh, *The Goldbergs* is the story of super geek and pop-culture fan Adam and his family, which includes mother Beverly, who believes her kids can do anything and will protect them at all costs; hardworking Murray, a dad who enjoys walking around in his underwear; confident middle brother Barry; popular older sister Erica; and of course, Adam's best friend and grandpa, Pops, who gives good advice and doesn't take anything too seriously.

Getting (and keeping) a girlfriend, learning how to do magic, auditioning for a part in the school play, and getting lost at a Phillies game are just some of the hurdles Adam tries to overcome with the help (and sometimes hindrance) of his parents and siblings. *The Goldbergs* has been praised by critics and viewers alike for bringing back life in the 1980s in such a colorful—and hysterical—fashion.

GENRE:
Sitcom

AGE:
14+

SEASONS:
4 and counting

STARRING:
Wendi McLendon-Covey, Sean Giambrone, George Segal, and Jeff Garlin

DID YOU KNOW?

Every season, the show does an episode inspired by a famous 80s movie. So far, *The Goonies*, *Ferris Bueller's Day Off*, and *A Christmas Story* have all been featured.

Saw it! ☐ Rating: ☆☆☆☆☆

Date: ___/___/_____ With: _____

Notes: _____

_____

22

THE DICK VAN DYKE SHOW

GENRE:
Sitcom

AGE:
7+

SEASONS:
5

MADE BY:
Carl Reiner

"It just so happens that you don't
know me as well as I know me, because
I'm with myself almost constantly."
—Rob Petrie

You may already know Dick Van Dyke from his movie roles in *Mary Poppins* and *Chitty Chitty Bang Bang*, but during the same time, this enormously talented actor, singer, dancer, and all-around funnyman was starring in a lovable sitcom.

The Dick Van Dyke Show was created by comic genius Carl Reiner and was partly based on his experience as a writer for *Your Show of Shows*, a variety show starring Sid Caesar. Van Dyke stars as Rob Petrie, head writer for a TV variety show. Mary Tyler Moore plays his wife, Laura, who wears capri pants and matches wits with Rob. They are vulnerable and loving characters who also stress out and obsess about little things, which leads to delightfully silly situations. In one great episode, Rob is convinced they brought the wrong baby home from the hospital. In another, he's convinced he's allergic to his family.

Rob and his staff spend the day writing skits, cracking jokes, mocking their producer, and trying to keep the show's difficult star happy. Much of *The Dick Van Dyke Show* takes place behind the scenes of a popular TV show where witty, creative people manage celebrities under the pressure of exhausting deadlines and show-biz kookiness. This sitcom feels fresher than others from the era because Rob and Laura are smart and sophisticated—and so is their humor.

STARRING:
Dick Van Dyke,
Mary Tyler Moore,
Rose Marie,
Morey Amsterdam,
and
Larry Mathews

NETWORK:
CBS

SPIN-OFFS
The Dick Van Dyke Show Revisited

DID YOU KNOW?
The network censors objected to Mary Tyler Moore wearing pants, and required her to wear dresses in most scenes—at least for the first few episodes!

Saw it! ☐ Rating: ☆☆☆☆☆
Date: ___/___/_____ With: _____
Notes: _____
_____

23

FAMILY MATTERS

GENRE:
Sitcom

AGE:
8+

SEASONS:
9

STARRING:
Reginald
VelJohnson,
Jo Marie Payton,
Darius McCrary,
Kellie Shanygne
Williams, and
Jaleel White

Carl Winslow, a Chicago police officer, lives in the suburbs with his wife, Harriette, and their children, Eddie, Laura, and Judy. Carl tries his best to keep his family strong by teaching his kids to work hard and have good values. He's the dad everyone wishes they had, with the perfect mix of wisdom, reason, discipline, and humor.

But there's one character that can make him lose his good humor—the bumbling super geek, Stephen Urkel. Sporting his glasses, suspenders, and high-waisted pants, Urkel is about the most annoying neighbor you could ever have, even though he always means well. He never stops professing his love for Laura, trying to be friends with Eddie, or annoying Carl. He's guilty of accidentally burning down the local teen hangout, waking up the entire neighborhood while serenading Laura, and somehow knocking both Carl and Eddie off the roof. But through all the antics and misadventures, the Winslows—and Steve Urkel—show us that family really does matter.

DID YOU KNOW?

Originally, Urkel was written to be in just one episode; but the audience reaction was so positive that he was written in as a regular. He also made guest appearances on *Step by Step*, *Full House*, and *Meego*.

Saw it! ☐   Rating: ☆☆☆☆☆
Date: ___/___/_____   With: _____
Notes: _____
_____

3RD ROCK FROM THE SUN

24

What if aliens landed on Earth, aka the third rock from the sun? Unlike the scary aliens we fear at the movies, the aliens that land on this show are ridiculous, utterly perplexed, and totally harmless.

John Lithgow plays Dick Solomon, the innocent commander who leads an expedition to Earth. He and his crew assume human forms and masquerade as a (very weird) family. Solomon assumes the form of a middle-aged man, but he's the youngest alien in his crew. Meanwhile Tommy, the eldest alien, assumes the body of a teenager, and has to deal with teen issues. The other "family members" are Sally, the second-in-command security officer, and Harry, the dim-witted communications officer.

Throughout the series, the gang tries to fit in, not blow their cover, and learn what they can about the human condition. Just like humans, these lovable aliens stumble through Earthling emotions. Whatever form they take, the crew on *3rd Rock* offers an unconventional, smart alternative in this down-to-earth sitcom.

GENRE:
Sitcom

AGE:
14+

SEASONS:
6

STARRING:
John Lithgow,
Kristen Johnston,
French Stewart,
Joseph Gordon-Levitt,
and
Jane Curtin

DID YOU KNOW?

3rd Rock from the Sun: The Official Report On Earth is a fictional book written by the Solomons about observations made during their stay on Earth.

Saw it! ☐ Rating: ☆☆☆☆☆
Date: ___ / ___ / _____ With: _____
Notes: _____

25

THE ADVENTURES OF OZZIE & HARRIET

GENRE:
Sitcom

AGE:
6+

SEASONS:
14

STARRING:
Ozzie Nelson,
Harriet Nelson,
David Nelson,
and
Ricky Nelson

Started as a radio show in 1952, *The Adventures of Ozzie & Harriet* eventually became the longest-running live-action sitcom on American television. With over 434 episodes, this all-American show became the gold standard for family television.

Essentially playing themselves, the Nelson family used their own real lives—even their home and their neighbors—as inspiration for new episodes. Ozzie is a bandleader and musician, and Harriet is his "girl singer;" their sons Ricky and David grow up in front of the cameras over the course of the show.

The show is known for depicting America in the "good old days," when every house had a white picket fence, your neighbors were your best friends, and all your spare time was spent at the the malt shop in town. It's a true classic and will always be remembered as a snapshot of the ideal 1950s American family.

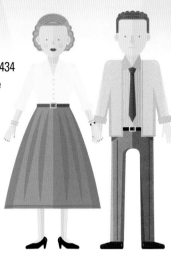

DID YOU KNOW?
The show blurred the lines between reality and fiction. When real-life Ricky wanted to become a drummer, the show featured an episode with the same theme. The teen's character performed the song "I'm Walkin,'" and Ricky sold a million real-life records that week!

SPIN-OFFS
Ozzie's Girls

Saw it! ☐ Rating: ☆☆☆☆☆
Date: ___/ ___/ _____ With: _____
Notes: _____
_____

iCARLY

iCarly is a show within a show. Webcasting from her makeshift, third-floor loft studio, Carly and her best friends, Sam and Freddie, accidentally create a show that becomes an online sensation and an international hit.

Carly is laid back, smart, and gifted with the ability to get out of nearly any sticky situation. She's also super-smart and pretty laid-back. Her best friend and co-host, Sam, comes from a slightly unusual family and loves to eat. Freddie, who lives across the hall, is the tech-producer for the show. He's got a crush on Carly, and he's close with Carly's older brother and legal guardian, Spencer.

Set in Seattle, the show deals with typical teen adventures, such as boyfriends, detention, mean teachers, and talent shows. The webcast adds another layer to the show, as Carly, Sam, and Freddie host contests, interview guests, and answer fan questions. The *iCarly* crew always keeps it funny!

The show was a favorite of the Kids' Choice and Teen Choice Awards, and was nominated for an Emmy for Outstanding Children's Program five times. As the first show to include content kids wrote in the scripts, *iCarly* is definitely a part of TV history too. iThink you are absolutely going to want to see *iCarly*!

SPIN-OFFS
Sam & Cat

GENRE:
Sitcom

AGE:
8+

SEASONS:
6

STARRING:
Miranda Cosgrove, Jerry Trainor, Jennette McCurdy, and Nathan Kress

DID YOU KNOW?
Every episode title starts with "i," such as "iMust Have Locker 239" and "iMight Switch Schools."

Saw it! ☐ Rating: ☆☆☆☆☆
Date: ___/___/_____ With: _____
Notes: _____
_____

27 ROSEANNE

GENRE:
Sitcom

AGE:
13+

SEASONS:
9

MADE BY:
Matt Williams
and
Roseanne Barr

Dan: Are you ever
sorry we got married?
Roseanne: Every second
of my life.
Dan: Me too.
Roseanne: You are, really?
Dan: [thinks] Nah.
Roseanne: OK,
me neither, then.

With nine seasons, four Emmys, three Golden Globes, four American Comedy Awards, a Peabody, and great ratings, *Roseanne* was a groundbreaking show. It was one of the first series about a struggling, working-class family, where both parents worked outside the home. It was also one of the first series to take a female perspective.

Roseanne is a big, brassy, hardworking woman with an in-your-face personality and a quick wit. The comedy follows the Conners, a loving couple with three kids. But *nothing* is sugar coated; the family fights and bickers, the parents yell at their kids, and the kids yell back. And these aren't just silly sitcom misunderstandings; the characters fight about important topics. But with all the stress, tension, and chaos, *Roseanne* manages to be a truly funny show.

Roseanne works on an assembly line and goes on to have a series of menial jobs, while her husband, Dan, works in construction. Roseanne's sister, Jackie, flounders to find a decent job and a suitable relationship. Daughter Darlene is a tomboy who refuses to conform to society's definition of a proper young lady. Her older sister Becky is an overachiever, but also a bit of a rebel, and eventually runs away with her biker boyfriend. DJ is the youngest. Paychecks are precarious, and money is always a concern. All the characters are cynical and sarcastic, but they also show each other real affection and loyalty, while cracking jokes and making fun of one another.

STARRING:
Roseanne Barr,
John Goodman,
Laurie Metcalf,
Sara Gilbert,
Michael
Fishman,
Alicia Goranson,
and
Sarah Chalke

NETWORK:
ABC

DID YOU KNOW?
Roseanne was filmed on the same stage as *Gilligan's Island*, *Mary Tyler Moore*, and *That 70s Show*!

Saw it! ☐   Rating: ☆☆☆☆☆
Date: ___/___/_____ With: _____
Notes: _____
_____

28

EVERYBODY HATES CHRIS

GENRE:
Sitcom

AGE:
12+

SEASONS:
4

STARRING:
Tyler James Williams,
Terry Crews,
Tichina Arnold,
Tequan Richmond,
Imani Hakim,
and
Vincent Martella

Like *The Wonder Years*, this show is narrated by an adult version of the main character, a plucky boy in middle school. But this show is about an urban African-American family, rather than a suburban white family, and the edgier tone reflects their difficult experiences.

Throughout the series, comedian Chris Rock brings his cynical sense of humor to his memories of childhood. And there's often a funny disparity between what young Chris tells his parents and what adult Chris Rock confesses to viewers.

Chris's strict parents, Julius and Rochelle, reprimand their kids, but they strive to keep them safe and honest while helping them steer clear of the crime that surrounds them. Chris's parents send him to a safer school two hours away, but whether he's there or in his neighborhood, his moral compass is always spinning as he encounters bullies, thieves, and police, as well as typical teen concerns. Some story lines include heavy topics, but Chris Rock's commentary always keeps each episode playful and fun. And lines like "I'll slap da caps off ya knees!" make the other characters just as memorable.

DID YOU KNOW?
The show is set in the 1980s, even though Chris Rock actually grew up the 1970s, because there were already so many shows set in the 1970s.

Saw it! ☐ Rating: ☆☆☆☆☆
Date: ___/___/_____ With: _____
Notes: _____
_____

THE ANDY GRIFFITH SHOW

Premiering in 1960, *The Andy Griffith Show* earned its place in TV history as the perfect depiction of life in a sleepy, small town in middle America.

The show follows widowed sheriff Andy Taylor and his young son, Opie, as they live their lives in the fictional town of Mayberry, North Carolina. It's Andy's job to deal with the town's troublemakers, and he always doles out justice fairly. Whatever the crime at hand, there are also plenty of laughs along the way, especially when bumbling deputy Barney is involved. Since not much crime happens in Mayberry, Andy has plenty of time on his hands to reflect and offer advice to the locals. He also loves taking Opie fishing and spending quiet evenings at home on the porch. Extremely popular throughout its eight-season run, *The Andy Griffith Show* influenced a generation of viewers, and has been on the air, between prime time and syndication, for more than 50 years!

GENRE:
Sitcom

AGE:
6+

SEASONS:
8

SPIN-OFFS

Gomer Pyle, U.S.M.C
Mayberry R.F.D.

DID YOU KNOW?

Unlike other sitcoms of its time, *The Andy Griffith Show* was filmed on location, rather than in a studio.

STARRING:
Andy Griffith,
Ron Howard,
and
Don Knotts

Saw it! ☐   Rating: ☆☆☆☆☆
Date: ___/___/_____   With: _____
Notes: _____
_____

30

MODERN FAMILY

GENRE:
Sitcom

AGE:
13+

SEASONS:
8 and counting

MADE BY:
Christopher
Lloyd and
Steven Levitan

"I've always said that if my son thinks of me as one of his idiot friends, I've succeeded as a dad."
—Phil Dunphy

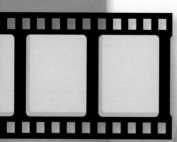

Today families may look a little different than they did 50 or 100 years ago. *Modern Family* highlights these differences for laughs, and the result is a thought provoking show for parents and kids who like to watch quality TV together.

Featuring smart writing and an A-list cast, *Modern Family* is a clever, goofy, character-based comedy. The show follows three very different households in the Pritchett family. Jay Pritchett is a curmudgeonly father of two adult children and a new baby, a stepfather, *and* a grandfather. His second wife, Gloria, a wise, strong-willed Colombian, is younger than Jay's own daughter and has a precocious son, Manny, from a previous marriage. Jay's eldest son, Mitchell, is married to Cam, and they have a daughter, Lily, whom they adopted from Vietnam. Mitchell's sister Claire is married to Phil Dunphy, and they have three kids: Haley, the popular one; Alex, the smart one; and Luke, the weird one.

This loving and hilariously imperfect brood represents a wide variety of marriage and parenting styles. Siblings Claire and Mitchell are tightly wound and rigid like their dad, while their partners Phil, Cam, and Gloria have much more fun-loving personalities. It's a lot to keep track of, but the memorable characters make it easy to get to know this family. With this show, 12 characters + 1 modern family = lots of laughs!

STARRING:
Ed O'Neill,
Sofía Vergara,
Julie Bowen,
Ty Burrell,
Jesse Tyler Ferguson,
Eric Stonestreet,
Sarah Hyland,
Ariel Winter,
Nolan Gould,
Rico Rodriguez,
and
Aubrey Anderson-Emmons

NETWORK:
ABC

DID YOU KNOW?
Each season of *Modern Family* features a vacation. The family has been to Disneyland, a dude ranch, Hawaii, and Las Vegas—and none of the trips have gone quite as planned!

Saw it! ☐   Rating: ☆☆☆☆☆
Date: ___/___/_____   With: _____
Notes: _____
_____

31

THE JEFFERSONS

GENRE:
Sitcom

AGE:
11+

SEASONS:
11

STARRING:
Isabel Sanford,
Sherman
Hemsley,
Marla Gibbs,
Roxie Roker,
Franklin Cover,
and
Paul Benedict

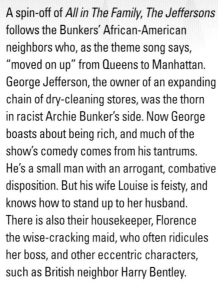

A spin-off of *All in The Family*, *The Jeffersons* follows the Bunkers' African-American neighbors who, as the theme song says, "moved on up" from Queens to Manhattan. George Jefferson, the owner of an expanding chain of dry-cleaning stores, was the thorn in racist Archie Bunker's side. Now George boasts about being rich, and much of the show's comedy comes from his tantrums. He's a small man with an arrogant, combative disposition. But his wife Louise is feisty, and knows how to stand up to her husband. There is also their housekeeper, Florence the wise-cracking maid, who often ridicules her boss, and other eccentric characters, such as British neighbor Harry Bentley.

The show frequently addresses issues of class and race, such as a prosperous African-American family being stereotyped as disadvantaged. Families watching

DID YOU KNOW?
George's neighbors, Helen and Tom Willis, were one of the first interracial couples on TV.

this show will also want to take time to talk about the uncensored use of racial expletives. But mostly, there's lots of light humor with typical sitcom misunderstandings.

Over 30 years after it first aired, it's still great to watch a show that features African-Americans and doesn't traffic in stereotypes, leading the way for everyone to "move on up."

SPIN-OFFS
Checking In

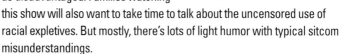

Saw it! ☐   Rating: ☆☆☆☆☆
Date: ___/___/_____ With: _____
Notes: _____
_____

FRESH OFF THE BOAT

One of the first prime-time shows to feature an Asian-American family, *Fresh Off the Boat* is based on actor/writer Eddie Huang's experiences growing up. Eddie's Taiwanese family relocates from Washington DC's Chinatown to Orlando, Florida in the 1990s to pursue the American Dream. But it's not as easy to fit in as they thought it would be.

   The show begins when Eddie is 11 years old. Everyone in the family is trying to make friends, win the respect of their new neighbors, and fit in with the community. Eddie's mother, Realtor and go-getter Jessica, runs the show, while dad Louis manages the family restaurant with spotty success. Eddie is a cool, confident guy who loves Biggie Smalls and rap. He wants his first school dance to be as awesome as a John Hughes movie, but sometimes his strict parents get in the way.

   Fresh Off the Boat is a hit with viewers, and was nominated for a slew of awards. The series pushes viewers to think about race, but this isn't just must-see TV because it's an important show—it's also hilarious to watch!

DID YOU KNOW?
The real Eddie Huang is a famous chef who owns BaoHaus, a Taiwanese bun restaurant in New York City.

GENRE:
Sitcom

AGE:
12+

SEASONS:
3 and counting

STARRING:
Randall Park,
Constance Wu,
and
Hudson Yang

Saw it! ☐ Rating: ☆☆☆☆☆
Date: ___/___/_____ With: _____
Notes: _____
_____

33

THE PARTRIDGE FAMILY

GENRE:
Sitcom

AGE:
7+

SEASONS:
4

MADE BY:
Bernard Slade

"C'mon, get happy!"
—From the classic theme song

If you liked *The Brady Bunch*, *The Partridge Family* is even groovier! This 1970s show is full of bell-bottom jeans, guitars, and eye-popping color schemes. The Partridges aren't just a family; they're a pop band fronted by shaggy-haired teen-heartthrob Keith Partridge. Also in the family band are headstrong Laurie, sarcastic Danny, the younger Chris and Tracy, and their single mom Shirley Partridge.

The show and the music offer fluffy fun. The family band tours in their iconic painted school bus, while girls chase behind after Keith. Life on the road often produces memorable mishaps, including the gang bathing in tomato juice when a skunk sprays them before a gig, or the kids trying to play matchmaker for their mother and their manager, Ruben. While the TV band's catchy songs were mostly lip-synced, their music was popular in real life and often played on the radio. Their hit song "I Think I Love You" reached Number 1 on the charts in 1970. Fan crushes, sibling rivalry, high-school shenanigans, coping with fame, and the band's career kept the show humming along for four happy seasons.

SPIN-OFFS

Partridge Family 2200 A.D.
Thanksgiving Reunion with The Partridge Family and My Three Sons

STARRING:
Shirley Jones, David Cassidy, Danny Bonaduce, Susan Dey, Suzanne Crough, Brian Forster, and Dave Madden

NETWORK:
ABC

DID YOU KNOW?

Real life mirrored art when teen heartthrob David Cassidy played fictional teen heartthrob Keith Partridge. Girls were gaga for both.

Saw it! ☐ Rating: ☆☆☆☆☆

Date: ___/___/_____ With: _____

Notes: _____

_____

34

PUNKY BREWSTER

GENRE:
Sitcom

AGE:
8+

SEASONS:
4

STARRING:
Soleil Moon Frye, George Gaynes, and Cherie Johnson

At just 8 years old, perky Penelope "Punky" Brewster is an orphan. Luckily, she meets Henry Warnimont, an elderly widower who's a bit grumpy, but grows to love Punky. Her best friend is 8-year-old Cherie Johnson, who lives upstairs with her grandmother Betty. She also loves to hang out with her friend Allen, who's a bit of a geek, and Margaux, who comes from a very wealthy family.

With her colorful wardrobe and persistently optimistic attitude, Punky looks at life through a rainbow-colored lens. Whether she's going fishing with Henry, having a sleepover with Cherie and Margaux, or going on an adventure with her dog, Brandon, Punky uses her "Punky Power" to brave any trouble that arises. And even though he's never raised a child, Henry does his best to be the kind of foster parent that Punky can be proud of. They may not have a family like everyone else's, but Punky and Henry prove that loyalty and love are what make a family work, as they teach each other about kindness, friendship, and making the best of any difficult situation.

SPIN-OFFS

It's Punky Brewster

DID YOU KNOW?
Candace Cameron (who plays D.J. in *Full House*) is in an episode of *Punky Brewster* as Punky's new neighbor.

Saw it! ☐   Rating: ☆☆☆☆☆
Date: ___/ ___/ _____ With: _____
Notes: _____
_____

WHO'S THE BOSS?

35

One of the most popular sitcoms of the 1980s, *Who's The Boss?* tells the story of a retired baseball player, Tony Micelli, and his daughter, Samantha, who come to live with a wealthy family in Connecticut. Tony applies to be busy advertising-executive Angela Bower's live-in housekeeper, and while at first she is thrown off by the idea of a guy cleaning her house, Angela warms to the idea once she sees how Tony gets along with her mom, Mona, and her son, Jonathan.

Over eight seasons, as Sam and Jonathan grow up, Tony and Angela create their own kind of family, even though they're not married. Tony's laid-back cool balances Angela's stricter, more uptight parenting style, and together, they make the perfect match. Together the family tackles big and small questions: *Will Sam be the next prima ballerina? Will Jonathan gain the confidence he needs? Is that a little romance brewing between Tony and Angela?* And *who really IS the boss in this family?* You'll have to watch to find out!

SPIN-OFFS
Living Dolls
Charmed Lives

GENRE:
Sitcom

AGE:
8+

SEASONS:
8

STARRING:
Tony Danza,
Judith Light,
Alyssa Milano,
Danny Pintauro,
and
Katherine
Helmond

DID YOU KNOW?
Versions of *Who's the Boss?* have been produced in several countries around the world, including England, France, Germany, Mexico, Italy, and Russia.

Saw it! ☐ Rating: ☆☆☆☆☆
Date: ___/___/_____ With: _____
Notes: _____

36 HAPPY DAYS

GENRE:
Sitcom

AGE:
7+

SEASONS:
11

MADE BY:
Gary Marshall

"Eyyy"
—Fonzie

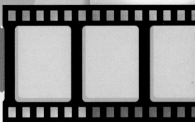

A nostalgic depiction of the 1950s, *Happy Days* was a long-running series that began airing in 1974. The show follows a group of all-American teenagers who hang out at Arnold's Drive-In, dance to the jukebox, and navigate dating, parents, and high school—while trying to appear as cool as possible.

Ron Howard plays Richie Cunningham, a wholesome, freckle-faced kid who is part of a typical, middle-class, suburban family. Throughout the series, he tries to balance being a good kid with being a socially successful teen. Since the show ran for almost a decade, its focus transformed from a charming look at youth culture to a broader comedy with more antics and bigger laughs. Richie hangs out with his best friends Potsie, Ralph, and a greaser named Fonzie. While the show revolves around Richie, his family, and friends, Fonzie, played by Henry Winkler, is the breakout star. Always wearing his white T-shirt and black leather jacket, Fonzie is the tough guy with a heart of gold. His success with the ladies is legendary, and his magical ability to whack a jukebox and make it play earns him a mythic reputation as the coolest of the cool. Though the show discusses difficult topics like racism and the Cold War, these subjects are addressed with a light touch. In this feel-good show, jokes and one-liners are always the priority.

STARRING:
Ron Howard,
Marion Ross,
Anson Williams,
Tom Bosley,
Henry Winkler,
Don Most, and
Erin Moran

NETWORK:
ABC

SPIN-OFFS
Laverne & Shirley
Blansky's Beauties
Mork & Mindy
Out of the Blue
Joanie Loves Chachi
The Fonz and the Happy Days Gang

DID YOU KNOW?
The Fonz became so popular that after the first few seasons, the network considered renaming the show *Fonzie's Happy Days* or *Fonzie*.

Saw it! ☐   Rating: ☆☆☆☆☆
Date: ___/___/_____   With: _____
Notes: _____
_____

37

MALCOLM IN THE MIDDLE

GENRE:
Sitcom

AGE:
13+

SEASONS:
7

STARRING:
Bryan Cranston,
Jane Kaczmarek,
and
Frankie Muniz

Malcolm has a photographic memory and an IQ of 165. But even a super-smart 10-year-old kid can have a dysfunctional family. His mom, Lois, is a teeny bit overbearing, while his dad, Hal, is a tad clueless. Malcolm is the middle child, and he and his family live in a typical American suburban neighborhood.

The show doesn't have a "laugh track," and it frequently allows the characters to "break the fourth wall" and address viewers directly through the camera. Malcolm's monologues give viewers insight into his "aha" moments and more details about his lovable and quirky family. He goes through what every American kid navigates: bullies, babysitting, pranks, and parental injustices. But he's also trying to contend with what it means to be a genius and how it sometimes stinks to be good at everything. Through it all, the family's unpredictable hijinks are hysterical.

The show received rave reviews and several Emmys at a time when everyone thought the classic sitcom was dead. A surprise hit, the show is now a time capsule for American family life in the early 2000s, and definitely deserves a spot on your must-see list!

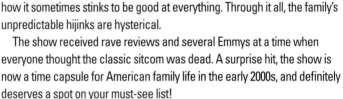

DID YOU KNOW?

Malcolm's family doesn't have an official last name. It was briefly mentioned as "Wilkerson" in the pilot episode, but it was never used again. Producers jokingly referred to them on set as the "Nolastname" family.

Saw it! ☐ Rating: ☆☆☆☆☆
Date: ___/___/_____ With: _____
Notes: _____
_____

LEAVE IT TO BEAVER

A black-and-white series that premiered in 1957, *Leave It to Beaver* is about a young boy and his family. Beaver's mom, June, is the perfect 1950s mom; she's constantly dressed up in high heels and pearls, even when she's cleaning the house, and she always seems to have a plate of cookies and milk available for the kids. Beaver's dad, Ward, works hard and doles out fair, reasonable discipline to his boys. Wally, Beaver's older brother, is a popular jock who often defends his little brother.

Leave It to Beaver was one of the first prime-time shows to be told from a kid's perspective. But *Leave It to Beaver* is truly a show about family; in most episodes, Beaver or Wally has a problem that June and Ward help with. Their adventures are captured with a sense of fun, and the show has proven to stand the test of time, with many fans, new and old, loving *Leave It to Beaver*.

DID YOU KNOW?

Theodore is called "Beaver" by his family because when Wally was younger, he tried saying "Theodore," and it came out sounding like "Beaver!"

GENRE:
Sitcom

AGE:
6+

SEASONS:
6

STARRING:
Barbara Billingsley,
Jerry Mathers,
Hugh Beaumont,
and
Tony Dow

Saw it! ☐ Rating: ☆☆☆☆☆
Date: ___ / ___ / _____ With: _____
Notes: _____
_____

39

FAMILY TIES

GENRE:
Sitcom

AGE:
11+

SEASONS:
7

MADE BY:
Gary David
Goldberg

"Mom, I need to reevaluate my life. Do you have a minute?"
—Mallory Keaton

The *Family Ties* premise gives traditional sitcoms a funny switcheroo. In the Keaton household, parents Steven and Elyse hope to share their liberal values with their kids, but instead they always seem to butt heads with their conservative son. While it's always light-hearted, this series demonstrates the clash between ideology from the 1960s and the 1980s.

Alex P. Keaton, the sweater-vest-and-tie-wearing teenager played by Michael J. Fox, gives the show its charm. Much of the plot revolves around Alex's plans to attend an Ivy League college and take over the world. He often mocks his sister, Mallory, who's more interested in boys and shopping than school and power. There's also youngest sister, Jennifer, and in the fifth season, Elyse gives birth to baby Andy. Amidst the comedy (much of it related to Alex's high-strung nature), the show tackles a lot of serious topics.

Unlike other 1980s sitcoms, *Family Ties* relies more on wit and character-based humor than punch lines, slapstick, and corny comedy. And viewers can rest easy knowing, while the Keatons clash over politics or quirks in personality, these family ties are strong enough to withstand any differences.

STARRING:
Meredith Baxter,
Michael Gross,
Michael J. Fox,
Justine Bateman,
Tina Yothers,
and
Brian Bonsall

NETWORK:
NBC

DID YOU KNOW?

The Keaton parents, Elyse and Steven, were originally conceived as the show's focus, but Michael J. Fox's charisma and humor stole the show.

Saw it! ☐ Rating: ☆☆☆☆☆

Date: ___/___/_____ With: _____

Notes: _____

_____

40

FULL HOUSE

GENRE:
Sitcom

AGE:
7+

SEASONS:
8

STARRING:
John Stamos,
Bob Saget,
Dave Coulier,
Candace
Cameron Bure,
Jodie Sweetin,
Mary-Kate Olsen,
Ashley Olsen,
and
Lori Loughlin

When Danny Tanner's wife dies in a tragic accident, he suddenly needs help raising his three daughters, D.J., Stephanie, and Michelle. His brother-in-law Jesse and best friend Joey move in, and the three men do their best to advise, guide, and support the three girls. And they have a whole lot of fun along the way!

Cool Uncle Jesse is a musician, Joey is a stand-up comedian, and Danny is a sportscaster who later becomes a morning talk-show host. The smart and practical D.J. (whose nickname is short for Donna Jo) is the oldest daughter. She's best friends with her next-door neighbor, Kimmy Gibbler. Sarcastic middle daughter Stephanie is a wee bit nosy, with a talent for snooping in her sister's business, and prone to exclaiming catchphrases like "How rude!" and "Hot dog!" Youngest daughter Michelle, played by famous twins Mary-Kate and Ashley Olsen, also has a ton of memorable catchphrases, including "You got it, dude!" and "You're in big trouble, mister!"

This show is a classic 1980s sitcom! Three men trying to take care of three growing girls leads to a bunch of misadventures and misunderstandings, but the bond between this family is truly touching.

SPIN-OFFS
Fuller House

DID YOU KNOW?
Though the show is set in San Francisco, it was filmed in Los Angeles. Only the opening credits and one episode in season eight were shot in San Fran!

Saw it! ☐   Rating: ☆☆☆☆☆
Date: ___/___/_____   With: _____
Notes: _____
_____

SHOW NO.

THE FACTS OF LIFE

41

The Facts of Life was one of the longest running sitcoms of the 1980s. Over nine seasons, the girls who live at Eastland Academy—a boarding school for girls—go through everything together, from falling in love to learning to drive. There's Blair, the rich, bratty girl; Jo, the tough girl from the Bronx; Natalie, the wide-eyed innocent one; and Tootie, the youngest who loves her roller skates. Watching over them is housemother Mrs. Garrett—former housekeeper from *Diff'rent Strokes*. She always has a hug and some seasoned advice to offer the girls.

The Facts of Life was also known for its more serious episodes, which tackle topics like drug abuse, eating disorders, and peer pressure. Through it all, the Eastland girls show us that friendship is the key to taking the bad with the good and being happy as you learn the facts of life.

DID YOU KNOW?

Two modern movie stars appeared on *The Facts of Life:* George Clooney and Molly Ringwald. And both were fired from the show!

GENRE: Sitcom

AGE: 11+

SEASONS: 9

STARRING: Charlotte Rae, Lisa Whelchel, Kim Fields, Mindy Cohn, and Nancy McKeon

Saw it! ☐ Rating: ☆☆☆☆☆

Date: ___/___/_____ With: ____________________

Notes: ________________________________

42

THE ADDAMS FAMILY

GENRE:
Sitcom

AGE:
8+

SEASONS:
2

STARRING:
Carolyn Jones,
John Astin,
Jackie Coogan,
Ted Cassidy,
Blossom Rock,
Ken Weatherwax,
and
Lisa Loring

As *The Addams Family's* memorable theme song explains, "they're creepy and they're kooky, mysterious and spooky, they're all together ooky…" *The Addams Family* was a refreshingly weird alternative to the sugary, all-American families of retro TV.

Inspired by characters created by *New Yorker* cartoonist Charles Addams, the black-and-white sitcom follows a ghoulish family and their eerie friends, including a butler who looks like Frankenstein; Cousin Itt, who is covered in hair; and a helpful, disembodied hand named Thing. The characters are as weird as can be, but the audience knows they mean no harm. Despite their macabre tastes, the family loves and supports one another. And they're kind to strangers, even if their hospitality might include scary touches like a bed of nails. This spooky series was short lived, but many years later it's still beloved by those who wandered into the Addams family's weird world.

DID YOU KNOW?
To make Cousin Itt's voice, the producer spoke gibberish into a tape recorder and played it back at a higher speed.

SPIN-OFFS

Addams Family Values
Addams Family Reunion
The Addams Family Broadway Musical
The New Addams Family

Saw it! ☐ Rating: ☆☆☆☆☆
Date: ___/___/_____ With: _____
Notes: _____
_____

THE MUNSTERS

The Munsters might seem like a copycat of *The Addams Family*, but in fact, the two series about ghoulish families aired at the same time, and *The Munsters* drew a larger audience. Both shows are a send-up of the corny all-American sitcoms of the previous decade. The characters differ though; the Addams are spooky and ooky humans, while the Munsters are actually supernatural.

Herman Munster is a lumbering, clumsy Frankenstein-style monster prone to temper tantrums. He drives a hearse and works as a gravedigger. His wife, Lily, manages the family and the household—sometimes with the help of a little magic. The couple, who married over a hundred years ago, live in a crumbling Victorian house on Mockingbird Lane with their son, Eddie; Lily's father, Sam Dracula; and Lily's niece, Marilyn. Like the Addams family, the Munsters don't understand why others are frightened of them, which of course means funny shenanigans ensue. The show's makeup and costumes are wonderfully fun, and the ghoulish humor tickles instead of chills the bones.

SPIN-OFFS

The Munsters Today
Munster, Go Home!
The Mini-Munsters
The Munsters' Revenge
Here Come the Munsters

GENRE:
Sitcom

AGE:
8+

SEASONS:
2

STARRING:
Fred Gwynne,
Yvonne De Carlo,
Al Lewis,
Pat Priest, and
Butch Patrick

Saw it! ☐ Rating: ☆☆☆☆☆
Date: ___ / ___ / _____ With: _____
Notes: _____
_____

44

I LOVE LUCY

GENRE:
Sitcom

AGE:
6+

SEASONS:
6

MADE BY:
Lucille Ball and
Desi Arnaz

DID YOU KNOW?
I Love Lucy has
never *not* been on
TV. New episodes
ran from 1951 to
1957 on CBS, and it
has aired
in syndication
ever since.

"Lucy, you got some
'splainin' to do!"
—Ricky Ricardo

People can't help going nuts for *I Love Lucy!* Many say it's the best sitcom of all time. While other black-and-white TV shows from the 1950s might seem stale or corny today, the comic genius of Lucille Ball has made her show a favorite for over 50 years.

The show featured Lucy and her real-life husband, Desi Arnaz, as Ricky Ricardo, a famous Cuban entertainer. William Frawley and Vivian Vance played Fred and Ethel Mertz, the Ricardos' best friends and neighbors. But the real star was Lucy's brilliant physical comedy. In one famous episode, Lucy and Ethel bet their husbands that going to work is easier than staying at home. They take a job in a chocolate factory but can't keep up with the assembly line that just keeps going faster and faster. When things go haywire, the chocolates start stacking up. They try stuffing them in their hats—and even in their mouths. The scene is totally ridiculous and unforgettably funny.

Many episodes centered on Lucy trying to trick or plead with Ricky into letting her do or buy something. But the show is also about friendship and being yourself, even when you're a bit of an odd ball. In the show, Lucy's cockamamie schemes often wind up backfiring. But hilarity always ensues! No laugh track needed.

In real life, Lucille Ball was a pioneering comedienne with an unsurpassed talent for slapstick and funny faces. But she was more than a clown. She was also a successful businesswoman and the first woman in television to lead a production company.

STARRING:
Lucille Ball,
Desi Arnaz,
William Frawley,
and
Vivian Vance

NETWORK:
CBS

SPIN-OFFS
The Lucy–Desi Comedy Hour
The Lucy Show
Here's Lucy
Life with Lucy

Saw it! ☐ Rating: ☆☆☆☆☆
Date: ___/ ___/ _____ With: _____
Notes: _____
_____

45

SAVED BY THE BELL

GENRE:
Sitcom

AGE:
9+

SEASONS:
4

STARRING:
Mark-Paul Gosselaar,
Mario Lopez,
Dustin Diamond,
Lark Voorhies,
Tiffani Theissen,
and
Elizabeth
Berkley

Saved by the Bell details the escapades of six high-school kids. Preppy Zack Morris is a charming guy who often speaks directly to the audience and has the uncanny ability to call "time out" and freeze everyone around him. Zack likes Kelly Kapowski, a super-popular, down-to-earth cheerleader who's great at pretty much everything. Then there's confident jock A.C. Slater. He's Zack's best friend, a star athlete, and boyfriend of Jesse Spano, a well-intentioned smarty pants and class president. Rounding out the crew are Lisa Turtle, a rich girl with a rad sense of fashion, and Screech, the resident geek.

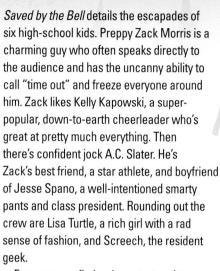

Everyone can find a character to relate to, and the crew's shenanigans are pretty hilarious. Favorite episodes include the gang pairing off into husband-and-wife teams for home-ec class, the students taking Mr. Belding's place as the principal, and a telethon at the friends' favorite diner. *Saved by the Bell*'s wild popularity make it one for the yearbooks!

SPIN-OFFS
Saved by the Bell: The College Years
Saved by the Bell: The New Class

DID YOU KNOW?
The set the show was filmed on still exists. It has also been used in shows like *That's So Raven* and *iCarly!*

Saw it! ☐ Rating: ☆☆☆☆☆
Date: ___/___/_____ With: _____
Notes: _____
_____

WELCOME BACK, KOTTER

In this 1970s series, Gabe Kotter returns to the inner-city high school of his youth to teach a group of unruly, remedial students called the "Sweathogs."

Based on star Gabe Kaplan's real-life experience as a student in a Brooklyn, New York school, the show features a variety of characters, all based on Kaplan's classmates; wise-cracking ladies' man Vinnie Barbarino is the leader of the pack, while Arnold Horshack is the jokester. Freddie "Boom Boom" Washington is the jock of the group, and Juan Epstein is small in stature but tough in nature. Kotter's job is to teach this group of "Sweathogs" more than just what's in the lesson plan; he also helps them sort out bad grades, disagreements, and their futures.

Welcome Back, Kotter features then-rising star John Travolta. Lunch boxes, action figures, and comic books were all created featuring the show's characters and punchlines. It's no wonder the show was such a hit; the Sweathogs and Mr. Kotter show us how some wise guys can actually learn some valuable (and hilarious) lessons from a great teacher.

GENRE:
Sitcom

AGE:
9+

SEASONS:
4

STARRING:
Gabe Kaplan,
Marcia
Strassman,
John Travolta,
Ron Palillo,
Robert Hegyes,
and
Lawrence
Hilton-Jacobs

DID YOU KNOW?

This show made the catchphrase "up your nose with a rubber hose" popular. It was one of Vinnie's many colorful comebacks.

Saw it! ☐ Rating: ☆☆☆☆☆

Date: ___ / ___ / _____ With: _____

Notes: _____

_____

47

GET SMART

GENRE:
Action &
Adventure

AGE:
10+

SEASONS:
5

STARRING:
Don Adams,
Barbara Feldon,
and
Edward Platt

Forever trying to foil the international organization of evil, KAOS, bumbling secret agent Maxwell Smart is always a split second away from disaster. Also known as Agent 86, Smart is on the case with Agent 99, his clever partner. Together they tackle villains and foil schemes working for CONTROL, a secret government agency in Washington, DC. They are aided by canine agent Fang—also known as Agent K-13—who loves to play with rubber ducks and turtlenecks.

The adventures of the agents always include a number of silly gadgets and secret weapons disguised as everyday objects like a ping-pong paddle, a cheese sandwich, or even an umbrella. There are secret passwords, top-secret documents, and dastardly villains. Whether they're protecting a princess, going undercover in outrageous disguises, or fighting off killer robots, with these spies, there is truly never a dull moment!

DID YOU KNOW?
Throughout its 138 episodes, the show features more than 50 different objects that are actually concealed phones, including Agent Smart's shoe phone!

Saw it! ☐   Rating: ☆☆☆☆☆
Date: ___/___/_____   With: _____
Notes: _____
_____

H2O: JUST ADD WATER

In *H2O: Just Add Water*, three best friends on the Gold Coast of Australia discover they have superpowers—whenever they come into contact with water, they transform into mermaids! This makes everyday life a bit more complicated, and the girls have to rely on each other to keep their new identities a secret.

Rikki, the new girl in town, can raise the temperature of water; Emma can freeze water; and Cleo can manipulate water into whatever form she wants. Lewis, Cleo's friend and science lover, tries to help the girls discover more about their powers, including how and why this happened to them.

Other than their new tails and scales, the girls are just like other 16-year-olds; they have to babysit their younger siblings, navigate the social hurdles of being invited (or uninvited) to parties, and try to avoid the humiliation of found diaries and botched karaoke parties.

H2O: Just Add Water has inspired fans all over the world. Exploring an underwater world through the eyes of magical mermaids? Who wouldn't love these fish tales!

SPIN-OFFS
Mako: Island of Secrets

DID YOU KNOW?
When wet, each mermaid tail weighs over 80 pounds! The actresses trained with experts to learn how to swim in their costumes.

GENRE:
Action & Adventure

AGE:
7+

SEASONS:
3

STARRING:
Cariba Heine,
Claire Holt,
and
Phoebe Tonkin

Saw it! ☐ Rating: ☆☆☆☆☆

Date: ___/___/_____ With: _____

Notes: _____

_____

49

DOCTOR WHO

GENRE:
Action &
Adventure

AGE:
10+

SEASONS:
26 and counting

MADE BY:
Sydney
Newman

"Do you wanna come with me? 'Cause if you do, then I should warn you, you're gonna see all sorts of things. Ghosts from the past; aliens from the future; the day the Earth died in a ball of flame; It won't be quiet, it won't be safe, and it won't be calm. But I'll tell you what it will be: the trip of a lifetime."
—The Ninth Doctor

Have you ever wished you could travel through space and time? With *Doctor Who*, you can! Doctor Who, an alien from the planet Gallifrey, travels in his stolen time-machine, or TARDIS, which stands for Time And Relative Distance In Space, and just happens to be camouflaged as a blue British call box from the 1950s.

The Doctor is passionately curious about Earth and humans. He travels through space and time trying to right wrongs, help others, and combat monsters and villains. He never uses a gun, but he does have a sonic screwdriver.

Twelve different actors have portrayed the Doctor; since Time Lords reincarnate, the Doctor takes on a new body (and perhaps some new personality quirks too) whenever he comes back from a "fatal" injury. Doctor Who typically has a human companion with him on his adventures, although sometimes he may bring a humanoid alien too. This companion helps remind Doctor Who of his "moral duty"—and sometimes causes trouble for him too.

The adventures of the Doctor are immensely popular, both in the UK and internationally. The show has inspired novels, video games, museum exhibits, and toys— even a pinball game! More than 800 episodes have been broadcast since the original show started in 1963, and there is no reason to think the Doctor's adventures will be ending anytime soon!

STARRING:
Matt Smith,
Peter Capaldi,
and
Jenna Coleman

NETWORK:
BBC

SPIN-OFFS

Torchwood
Totally Doctor Who
The Sarah Jane Adventures

DID YOU KNOW?
The show's popularity is so much a part of pop culture that the word *TARDIS* is now included in the Shorter Oxford English Dictionary!

Saw it! ☐ Rating: ☆☆☆☆☆

Date: ___ / ___ / _____ With: _____

Notes: _____

_____

50

BATMAN

GENRE:
Action & Adventure

AGE:
9+

SEASONS:
3

MADE BY:
Based on the characters created by Bob Kane and Bill Finger

"Quick! To the Batmobile!"
—Batman

Almost everyone knows about Batman: the legend, the comic book, the blockbuster films. But way back in the 1960s, the cape crusader and his sidekick, Robin, appeared in a campy live-action TV series that was way more light-hearted than the intense encounters the Dark Knight faces today. Starring Adam West as a squeaky-clean Batman and Burt Ward as Robin, the wide-eyed boy wonder, the series aired on ABC from 1966 to 1968.

Unlike other superheroes, Batman doesn't have any superpowers. He's just super awesome and super smart. Mix in an arsenal of super cool bat-gadgets and secret identities, and the show gets really exciting. The villains are criminals with goofy names like The Joker, The Penguin, Cat Woman, and Egg Head. Fight scenes are sprinkled with words like *KLONK, KAPOW, POWIE, THWACK,* and *VRONK*! Modern satires like *Austin Powers* mimic *Batman's* absurdity, like when the villain plots the hero's elaborate and totally escapable death. In one episode, Batman is attacked by an exploding shark, but he's saved by the Boy Wonder and a can of shark repellent. In another over-the-top pickle, Mr. Freeze tries to turn Batman and Robin into giant Sno-Cones. The series appeals to all ages; adults and older kids will appreciate the humor, while younger kids will love the candy-coated, high-octane action.

STARRING:
Adam West,
Burt Ward,
Alan Napier, and
Neil Hamilton

NETWORK:
ABC

DID YOU KNOW?
Robin the Boy Wonder exclaimed over 300 creative variations of "Holy," including "Holy Trampoline," "Holy Unknown Flying Object," and "Holy Fate-Worse-than-Death!"

SPIN-OFFS
Batman: The Animated Series
The Batman

Saw it! ☐   Rating: ☆☆☆☆☆
Date: ___/___/_____ With: _____
Notes: _____
_____

51

THUNDERBIRDS

GENRE:
Action &
Adventure

AGE:
7+

SEASONS:
2

STARRING:
Peter Dyneley,
Shane Rimmer,
Matt
Zimmerman,
Ray Barrett,
David Holliday,
Sylvia Anderson,
and
David Graham

Premiering in 1965, and set in 2065, this British sci-fi series features human-like puppets as the Tracys, a family who created the top-secret organization International Rescue (IR). IR is dedicated to saving human lives, with the help of their hi-tech machines, Thunderbirds.

Former astronaut Jeff Tracy has five adult sons. Scott pilots Thunderbird 1, a hypersonic rocket; Virgil pilots Thunderbird 2, a supersonic carrier; Alan and John pilot Thunderbird 3, a spacecraft, and Thunderbird 5, the space station; and Gordon pilots Thunderbird 4, a submersible. Lady Penelope Creighton-Ward, who leads a group of secret agents connected to IR and drives a pink Rolls Royce, and an engineer named Brains also join in the Thunderbird adventures. Together, they rescue those in need and save the world, all the while showcasing the amazing abilities of their machinery. Whether they are rescuing soldiers from a blazing pit, saving solarnauts from deadly radiation, or stopping the detonation of an atomic bomb, the Tracys are on the case. Viewers are sure to find this show totally FAB!

SPIN-OFFS
Thunderbirds Are Go

DID YOU KNOW?
The Tracy brothers are named after five of the "Original 7" American astronauts: Alan Shepard, Gordon Cooper, John Glenn, Scott Carpenter, and Virgil Grissom.

Saw it! ☐ Rating: ☆☆☆☆☆
Date: ___/___/_____ With: _____
Notes: _____
_____

MACGYVER

MacGyver is a secret agent who refuses to carry a gun—but he's so smart that he doesn't need it to outwit the bad guys. He just needs his trusty Swiss Army knife, a roll of duct tape, good ol' scientific logic, and his uncanny ability to use everyday items to create extraordinary solutions. The fact that he speaks a bunch of languages and knows everything there is to know about chemistry, technology, and physics helps too.

MacGyver can rig pretty much anything—shorting out a missile timer with a paper clip, making dynamite with salt and sugar, using a paper map as both a sled and a hot-air-balloon patch, and even fixing a blown fuse with a wad of chewing gum. While his missions are always harrowing, MacGyver's level-headed calm helps him avert danger and bring the bad guys to justice.

MacGyver's ability to make something out of nothing has become known in popular culture as "MacGyvering" it.

GENRE:
Action & Adventure

AGE:
11+

SEASONS:
7

STARRING:
Richard Dean Anderson and Dana Elcar

DID YOU KNOW?
Saturday Night Live did a parody skit of the show called "MacGruber," which went on to become a feature film in 2010.

Saw it! ☐   Rating: ☆☆☆☆☆
Date: ___/___/_____   With: _____
Notes: _____
_____

53

BUFFY THE VAMPIRE SLAYER

GENRE:
Action & Adventure

AGE:
13+

SEASONS:
7

MADE BY:
Joss Whedon

"Sure.
We saved the
world. I say
we party.
I mean, I got
all pretty."
-Buffy Summers

Sarah Michelle Gellar plays Buffy, a high-school student who discovers she's the "chosen one" tasked with protecting the world from vampires and demons. Besides being an awesome slayer, Buffy is a regular teenage girl with regular problems. She befriends Xander, the witty, geeky kid who offers comic relief, and Willow, a shy straight-A student with magical powers. They call themselves the "Scooby Gang," because they work together to battle the forces of evil—something that happens often since Sunnydale High School sits on top of a portal to the demon world. Total bummer!

While the episodes are often grisly, the show works on many levels. Story lines include a tumultuous relationship with a vampire, Willow's journey into witchcraft, and Buffy meeting other slayers. One part supernatural adventure, and one part comedy (with a lot of romantic drama mixed in), the series is about more than winning the war against demons. It's about surviving being a teenager, which can be just as monstrous.

SPIN-OFFS
Angel

STARRING:
Sarah Michelle Gellar, Nicholas Brendon, Alyson Hannigan, Charisma Carpenter, and Anthony Stewart Head

NETWORK:
The WB, UPN

DID YOU KNOW?
Buffy the Vampire Slayer has become a legitimate area of academic study known as Buffy Studies. Books, conferences, and dissertations have examined the show from the perspective of philosophy, religion, gender, linguistics, and more.

Saw it! ☐ Rating: ☆☆☆☆☆

Date: ___/___/_____ With: _____

Notes: _____

_____

54

WONDER WOMAN

GENRE:
Action & Adventure

AGE:
7+

SEASONS:
3

MADE BY:
William Moulton Marston and Stanley Ralph Ross

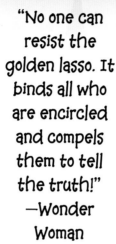

"No one can resist the golden lasso. It binds all who are encircled and compels them to tell the truth!"
—Wonder Woman

During World War II in the 1940s, Major Steve Trevor crashes his plane on Paradise Island in the Bermuda Triangle. He is discovered by an Amazon princess, Diana, who's compelled to return to America with him to fight against the Nazis and help the United States win the war. And so Wonder Woman is born!

Based on the wildly popular comic-book character, Wonder Woman is practically unstoppable. With bullet-deflecting bracelets, a boomerang tiara, a lasso of truth, and an invisible jet at her disposal, who can defeat her? Disguised as Major Trevor's secretary, Diana Prince keeps her Wonder Woman superpowers a secret, but twirls to transform into her alter ego whenever evil needs to be defeated—or whenever Steve is in trouble. Recovering stolen secrets from the Nazis, thwarting bank robbers, and diverting hijacked missiles are all in a day's work for Wonder Woman.

The first season of the TV series closely followed the comic books, but when the series moved to its second and third seasons, the setting was updated to the 1970s. The series went on to air in syndication throughout the 1980s, and was popular with viewers of all ages, who enjoyed the campy fun of the show. The theme song says: "Wonder Woman! All the world is waiting for you and the powers you possess! In your satin tights, fighting for your rights and the old red, white, and blue!" Surely, this is a show to salute!

STARRING:
Lynda Carter
and
Lyle Waggoner

NETWORK:
ABC, CBS

DID YOU KNOW?
Wonder Woman's metal bracelets are made from a material called "Feminum"!

Saw it! ☐ Rating: ☆☆☆☆☆

Date: ___/___/_____ With: _____

Notes: _____

_____

55 STAR TREK

GENRE:
Action & Adventure

AGE:
8+

SEASONS:
3

MADE BY:
Gene Roddenberry

"Space, the final frontier. These are the voyages of the starship Enterprise. Its five-year mission: to explore strange new worlds, to seek out new life and new civilizations, to boldly go where no man has gone before."
—Captain Kirk in the opening sequence

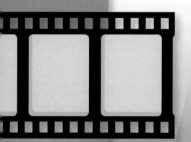

Probably the most iconic science-fiction TV show of our time, *Star Trek* is a must-see for anyone who is curious what the future might hold. Exploring new galaxies and planets and discovering new life forms are the sci-fi elements that draw viewers in. But it's the relationships between the members of the crew and creatures from other planets that lie at the heart of the show.

Star Trek's optimistic glimpse into the future shows a world where exploration is valued and all things are possible. With cool gadgets like the universal translator, handheld communicators, and the phaser gun, Captain Kirk and his crew inspired the imaginations of viewers all over the world—so much so, that many of these "far-fetched" imaginary gadgets now exist today!

Though the show never had particularly high ratings, it did have legions of dedicated and vocal fans called "Trekkies," who enthusiastically supported the show and demanded to see more of its characters. So while the original series only lasted for three seasons, the *Star Trek* world evolved into numerous full-length movies, spin-off TV series, and most recently, a reboot series of movies that reimagines the original characters.

The adventures of the starship *Enterprise* are now legendary, and the show is considered a cult classic; Captain Kirk, Mr. Spock, and the rest of the crew are so well known that viewers of all generations are boldly going where no one has gone before!

STARRING:
William Shatner,
Leonard Nimoy,
DeForest Kelley,
Nichelle Nichols,
James Doohan,
and
George Takei

NETWORK:
NBC

SPIN-OFFS

Star Trek: The Next Generation
Star Trek: Voyager
Deep Space Nine
Enterprise
Star-Trek: Discovery

DID YOU KNOW?
NASA is working on making the warp-drive technology featured in *Star Trek* real!

Saw it! ☐   Rating: ☆☆☆☆☆

Date: ___/___/_____ With: _____

Notes: _____

_____

56

MIGHTY MORPHIN' POWER RANGERS

GENRE:
Action & Adventure

AGE:
7+

SEASONS:
3

STARRING:
Richard Steven Horvitz,
Ed Neil,
David Yost,
David J. Fielding,
Amy Jo Johnson,
and
Thuy Trang

Do you have the Power in you? The Power Rangers phenomenon began in 1993 with the debut of the *Mighty Morphin' Power Rangers*. The show is adapted from the Japanese TV series *Super Sentai*, and uses much of the original Japanese footage. Episodes revolve around a team of five "teenagers with attitude" recruited by the wizard Zordon. He morphs them into superheroes with amazing abilities to fight against a witch named Rita Repulsa and the evil Lord Zedd. Each Ranger possesses a colorful, tight-fitting suit, a superhuman skill, and a special weapon.

It's not all teamwork and drop kicks though. These tough teens can never use their powers for their own personal gain or show their powers to the public, or they risk losing their abilities.

While these teens are dealing with the normal trials and tribulations of other high schoolers, they also have to worry about saving the universe. Football and cheerleading tryouts, getting good grades, and having crushes are all mixed up with navigating force fields, fighting super-sized monsters, and avoiding timeholes. Intergalactic battles, epic fights, and zippy dialogue are the hallmarks of the *Power Rangers*, making any time spent with them a whole lot of spacey, colorful fun!

DID YOU KNOW?
Fans who can't get enough *Power Rangers* attend the annual convention known as the Power Morphicon!

Saw it! ☐ Rating: ☆☆☆☆☆

Date: ___/___/_____ With: _____

Notes: _____

_____

GOOSEBUMPS

Based on the best-selling horror book series of the same name, *Goosebumps* is a collection of spooky stories about kids who find themselves in supernatural situations. For readers who loved R.L. Stine's original *Goosebumps* books, several titles were transformed into episodes, including such frightful tales as "Return of the Mummy," "The Girl Who Cried Monster," "Let's Get Invisible," and "Ghost Beach."

Ready to get thrilled and chilled? Each creepy installment of the TV show offers some spine-tingling twists, from chasing monsters to a haunted summer camp and a magical mask with questionable powers. The kids in each episode have to follow the clues to solve these mystical mysteries and overcome their darkest fears, while viewers are along for the ride. "Viewer beware, you're in for a scare!" says the narrator, warning viewers of the scary tales ahead. Sometimes gross and goofy, sometimes thrillingly terrifying, the *Goosebumps* adventures are sure to leave you delightfully frightened. Some braveness required!

GENRE:
Action & Adventure

AGE:
10+

SEASONS:
4

STARRING:
R.L. Stine

DID YOU KNOW?
The man in black carrying a briefcase in the opening sequence is author R.L. Stine.

Saw it! ☐ Rating: ☆☆☆☆☆

Date: ___ / ___ / _____ With: _____

Notes: _____

_____

58

THE TWILIGHT ZONE

GENRE:
Action & Adventure

AGE:
10+

SEASONS:
5

MADE BY:
Rod Serling

"You're traveling through another dimension, a dimension not only of sight and sound but of mind. A journey into a wondrous land whose boundaries are that of imagination. That's the signpost up ahead: your next stop, the Twilight zone!"
—From the opening narration of the show

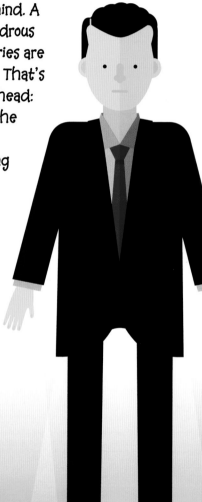

What happens when regular people are affected by extraordinary circumstances? They have entered the Twilight Zone! Each episode tells a different tale; unlike other shows that tell the story of a group of characters over time, this show features a completely new story and new characters in every episode. The only constant is narrator and creator Rod Serling, who introduces and closes each episode with some wise insights for viewers. Several well-known actors appear on the show, including William Shatner and Leonard Nimoy of *Star Trek*, movie stars Burt Reynolds and Robert Redford, and funny lady Carol Burnett.

Supernatural events, encounters with aliens, robots who seem human, time travel, and glimpses into the future are all reality in *The Twilight Zone*. Each episode's characters learn a valuable moral lesson in the end; most endings are a surprise or contain a twist the viewers wouldn't see coming.

Unlike anything else that was on air at the time, the show mixed fantasy, reality, and unpredictability, which made viewers tune in each week. Who would star in this week's episode? Would it be set in space or in someone's backyard? Which parts would be fantastic, and which would be so real you knew it could happen to you? Once you get a glimpse of the "fifth dimension," you'll want to see everything!

STARRING:
Rod Serling

NETWORK:
CBS

SPIN-OFFS
The Twilight Zone (1985)
The Twilight Zone (2002)

DID YOU KNOW?
Ray Bradbury, the great sci-fi author, wrote an episode of *The Twilight Zone*.

Saw it! ☐ Rating: ☆☆☆☆☆
Date: ___/___/_____ With: _____
Notes: _____
_____

SHOW NO.

59

SCOOBY-DOO, WHERE ARE YOU!

GENRE:
Animated
Adventure

AGE:
5+

SEASONS:
2

MADE BY:
William Hanna
and
Joseph Barbera

"And I would have gotten away with it, too, if it wasn't for you meddling kids."
—Classic Scooby-Doo villains

Long before Ghostbusters, a group of teenage friends and their dog Scooby-Doo chased ghosts, vampires, witches, and other spooky creatures in this Saturday morning cartoon. Four California high-school students drive around in a groovy green van called The Mystery Machine to solve mysteries. The supernatural spooks they chase always turn out to be regular human villains in disguise.

Shaggy is the slacker beatnik who has a scruffy goatee and says "like" a lot. Scooby-Doo is his dog, and together they're a lazy, cowardly, and comically hungry crime-solving duo. The rest of the gang includes Velma, the brainy one, who is always losing her glasses; Fred, the blond, handsome one, who wears an ascot and looks a little like a Ken doll; and the fashionable redhead Daphne, whose nickname is "Danger Prone Daphne," since she often needs rescuing. Together the gang works to prove what at first appears to be supernatural mysteries are actually simple hoaxes. Along the way, there are always chills, thrills, and plenty of laughs. The show premiered in 1969, following *The Archies*; *Scooby-Doo* mimicked *The Archies* simple cartoon style to appeal to the same teen audience. Today the biggest draws are still the silly, sweet Scooby-Doo and the fun of watching the gang solving a mystery in every episode. *Zoinks!*

STARRING:
Don Messick,
Casey Kasem,
Frank Welker,
Nicole Jaffe,
Stefanianna
Christopherson,
and
Heather North

NETWORK:
CBS, ABC

SPIN-OFFS

A Pup Named Scooby-Doo
The New Scooby-Doo Movies
Scooby's All-Star Laff-A-Lympics
Scooby-Doo Goes Hollywood
What's New, Scooby-Doo?
Scooby-Doo! Mystery
Incorporated

DID YOU KNOW?

The show's theme song has been covered by a number of famous artists, including Matthew Sweet, Third Eye Blind, The B-52s, and Billy Ray Cyrus.

Saw it! ☐   Rating: ☆☆☆☆☆
Date: ___/___/_____ With: _____
Notes: _____
_____

60

POPEYE THE SAILOR

GENRE:
Animated
Adventure

AGE:
5+

SEASONS:
2

STARRING:
Jack Mercer,
Mae Questel,
and
Jackson Beck

Popeye, the sailor man, has been guzzling spinach for over 85 years. He and his gangly gal pal Olive Oyl have appeared in comic strips, books, cartoons, radio segments, movie shorts, and films. When the old movie shorts from the 1930s, 1940s, and 1950s were broadcast on TV in the 1960s, viewer enthusiasm prompted a new series of made-for-television cartoons. The iconic characters remained the same, with Popeye getting out of a pickle by guzzling his spinach and brandishing his biceps in each episode.

The series is a mash-up of styles, plotlines, and spoofs. There are moments of Loony-Tunes-style hijinks and slapstick, and lots of fanciful elements, including shape-shifting and invisibility. The story lines range from competitions to more imaginative concepts, like when Popeye's prehistoric ancestors discover spinach. Other episodes feature arch-enemy Brutus putting Popeye in a machine that turns him into a baby. There are also Egyptian tombs, sunken treasure, fortune tellers, and bull fighting. But through it all, Popeye always wears his bright white navy duds, and manages to save the day!

DID YOU KNOW?
Popeye's love of spinach inspired adults and children to eat more spinach during the Great Depression!

Saw it! ☐ Rating: ☆☆☆☆☆

Date: ___ / ___ / _____ With: _____

Notes: _____

_____

SPEED RACER

Go, Speed Racer, Go! Speed Racer is just 18, and while he may be the youngest driver on the circuit, he's got the talent to go, go, go far.

Based on the Japanese manga series *Mach GoGoGo, Speed Racer* first came to American TV screens in 1967. Speed Racer drives the Mach 5, a super sweet race car that's said to be modeled after three real-life speed mobiles: the Aston Martin, the Ford GT40, and the Ferrari Testarossa. Speed's girlfriend, Trixie, a helicopter and airplane pilot, often accompanies him on his adventures, as does his brother, Spritle, and his pet chimpanzee, Chim-Chim. Masked Racer X drives Car 9 (also called the Shooting Star). He's an excellent driver, yet remains a mystery to Speed.

Speed always tries to do the right thing, whether he's competing in a race against Captain Terror and his Car Acrobatic Team, trying to defeat international spies, or foiling an assassination attempt. Speed's adventures are never short on fun or intrigue, and the style of the animation is colorful and bright, much like the manga series it's based on. Once you get hooked on the adventures of Speed Racer and his friends, you'll be pulling for him to win every race and defeat every villain.

DID YOU KNOW?
Trixie's name in the original Japanese series is Michi Shimura, which is why her shirt has an *M* on it.

GENRE:
Animated
Adventure

AGE:
6+

SEASONS:
1

STARRING:
Peter Fernandez,
Katsuji Mori,
and
Jack Grimes

Saw it! ☐   Rating: ☆☆☆☆☆
Date: ___ / ___ / _____   With: _____
Notes: _____
_____

62 RUGRATS

GENRE:
Animated Adventure

AGE:
6+

SEASONS:
10

STARRING:
Elizabeth Daily, Christine Cavanaugh, Kath Soucie, and Cheryl Chase

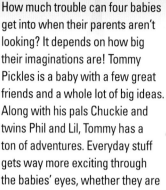

How much trouble can four babies get into when their parents aren't looking? It depends on how big their imaginations are! Tommy Pickles is a baby with a few great friends and a whole lot of big ideas. Along with his pals Chuckie and twins Phil and Lil, Tommy has a ton of adventures. Everyday stuff gets way more exciting through the babies' eyes, whether they are listening to tall tales from Tommy's Grandpa, avoiding naughty girl Angelica's attempts to scare them, or tackling vertigo on the big kids' slide. They always find a way to make everything into an adventure from their own unique point of view.

Inspired by their two small sons, creators Gábor Csupó and Arlene Klasky thought it would be cool to imagine what babies would say if they could talk and explore why they do all the silly things they do every day. While originally planned to appeal to kids, the show eventually became a hit with adults too. *Rugrats* was such a popular show that it inspired several specials, three feature films, and a bunch of cool collectibles, including pajamas, games, toys, and comics. No matter what age you are, you'll go gaga for this show!

DID YOU KNOW?
Until *SpongeBob SquarePants* came along, *Rugrats* was the longest running cartoon on Nickelodeon!

Saw it! ☐ Rating: ☆☆☆☆☆
Date: ___/___/_____ With: _____
Notes: _____
_____

POKÉMON

SHOW NO. 63

Based on a super-popular Japanese video game, the anime series *Pokémon* is a worldwide phenomenon. The series follows 10-year-old Ash, who can't wait to become a Pokémon (or Pocket Monster) master. Ash's main Pokémon is Pikachu, a small, yellow, mouse-like creature who has the power to attack its adversaries with electricity. Training for the Pokémon league, Ash and Pikachu gradually learn to trust one another, as they battle other Pokémon and their masters. Along the way, they make new friends, like gym leaders Misty and Brock, artist Tracey, and Pokémon coordinator May. Ash and his friends find new adventures in every episode, whether they are traveling through Neon City, where everyone is sleep-deprived and cranky, or journeying through the Orange Islands, making new friends and meeting mysterious creatures. There is always excitement to be found and more tests to be passed on Ash's way to becoming a master.

Pokémania recently surged again when the Pokémon Go app took the world by storm. With 19 seasons, you've got plenty of episodes to start watching. Gotta go catch 'em all!

SPIN-OFFS

Pokémon Chronicles
Pokémon Origins

DID YOU KNOW?

Pokémon legend states that Pikachu's name comes from a mash-up of two Japanese words: *pika* for the sound made when electricity sparks, and *chu* for the squeaky noise a mouse makes.

GENRE:
Animated Adventure

AGE:
6+

SEASONS:
19 and counting

STARRING:
Ikue Otani, Rodger Parsons, and Sarah Natochenny

Saw it! ☐ Rating: ☆☆☆☆☆

Date: ___/___/_____ With: ____________________

Notes: ____________________

____

64

SPIDER-MAN AND HIS AMAZING FRIENDS

GENRE:
Animated
Adventure

AGE:
6+

SEASONS:
3

MADE BY:
Stan Lee,
Jack Kirby,
and
Steve Ditko

"Firestar,
honey,
I lava you."
—Iceman

Are your Spidey senses tingling? They should be—Spider-Man and his friends Iceman and Firestar are here to save the day! Fighting villains across the globe, these Spider-Friends combine their superpowers to create a team to fight bad guys. By day, Peter Parker, Bobby Drake, and Anjelica Jones are all college students at Empire State University, living together with Peter's Aunt May. But when evil shows up, the three friends use their superpowers to defeat the supervillains.

This show introduces us to some awesome characters in the Marvel world, including Lightwave, who can control light, and Videoman, who is made of energy from a video arcade. Other more familiar X-Men also appear in the series, including Professor X, Magneto, Cyclops, Storm, and Wolverine. Together, the Spider-Friends try to foil the evil plots of the Beetle, the Shocker, the Chameleon, Electro, Green Goblin, and Mysterio. There's even an episode narrated by creator Stan Lee, and another that features a cameo from Marvel icon Iron Man.

Although *Spider-Man and His Amazing Friends* was only on TV for three seasons, the adventures of the Spider-Friends are definitely worth checking out. They're not just superheroes saving the planet; they're also good friends who have fun hanging out together whether they're battling a supervillain or goofing around at a superhero costume party.

STARRING:
Dan Gilvezan,
Frank Welker,
and
Kathy Garver

NETWORK:
NBC

DID YOU KNOW?

The Marvel character Human Torch was not available for this series due to legal issues, so the Marvel team created Firestar, a brand new character with similar powers.

Saw it! ☐ Rating: ☆☆☆☆☆
Date: ___/___/_____ With: _____
Notes: _____
_____

65

FOSTER'S HOME FOR IMAGINARY FRIENDS

GENRE:
Animated
Adventure

AGE:
7+

SEASONS:
6

STARRING:
Sean Marquette,
Grey Griffin,
and
Keith Ferguson

Have you ever wondered what happened to your old imaginary friends once you outgrew them? Chances are, they're living at Foster's Home for Imaginary Friends, an adoption center for outgrown imaginary pals.

The series revolves around eight-year-old Mac, who initially thinks he's outgrown Blooregard Q. Kazoo, a security blanket also known as Bloo, but later realizes he doesn't want to be without him. Mac talks old Madame Foster, proprietor of the Home, into letting Bloo stay there forever, as long as he comes to visit every day. During these visits, Mac encounters all kinds of castoff imaginary friend creatures waiting to be adopted by kids who can't think up their own imaginary friends, including Coco, an airplane-bird-palm tree hybrid who lays colorful eggs; Eduardo, a huge purple guy with horns and big teeth (who's actually kind of shy); and Wilt, a tall, red basketball player with just one arm. A world where kids and imaginary friends can stay together is pretty awesome, and you'll love seeing what kind of shenanigans Mac, Bloo, and the rest of the crew get into!

DID YOU KNOW?

Creator Craig McCracken, who also developed *The Powerpuff Girls*, reportedly got the idea for *Foster's* after adopting a shelter dog.

Saw it! ☐ Rating: ☆☆☆☆☆
Date: ___/___/_____ With: _____
Notes: _____
_____

AVATAR: THE LAST AIRBENDER

66

What if you were the only one who could save the world? That's what 12-year-old Aang is faced with when he realizes he is the chosen one and must fight to fix his war-torn world. There are four nations: The Fire Nation, The Water Tribes, The Earth Kingdom, and the Air Nomads. "Benders" of each nation can control, or bend, their own element through a combination of innate talent and magic. An Avatar is the only one who can bend all four elements, and there's only one Avatar in the whole world: Aang.

When we meet Aang, he has just been discovered hibernating in an iceberg by young Waterbender Katara and her elder brother Sokka from the Southern Tribe. Aang learns the world is out of balance since the Fire Nation attacked 100 years ago, sparking a global war. Together, they train to bend the elements and experience incredible adventures as they try to destroy the Fire Lord.

Aang's journey is spellbinding, with new twists and turns in every episode. The inspiring characters, intricate plots, and unique magical universe make *The Last Airbender* a must-see on your TV show list!

SPIN-OFFS
The Legend of Korra

GENRE:
Animated
Adventure

AGE:
8+

SEASONS:
3

STARRING:
Zach Tyler,
Mae Whitman,
and
Jack DeSena

DID YOU KNOW?
Each bending style is based on a different style of Chinese martial arts, including *tai chi* and *ba gua*.

Saw it! ☐ Rating: ☆☆☆☆☆
Date: ___ / ___ / _____ With: _____
Notes: _____
_____

67

TEENAGE MUTANT NINJA TURTLES

GENRE:
Animated
Adventure

AGE:
7+

SEASONS:
10

MADE BY:
Kevin Eastman
and
Peter Laird

"Turtle power! They're the world's most fearsome fighting team! They're heroes in a half-shell, and they're green!"
—From the classic theme song

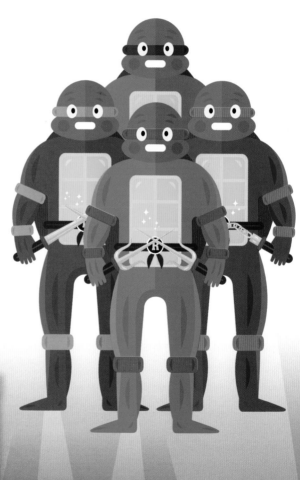

Creators Kevin Eastman and Peter Laird were starving artists when they came up with the idea for the *Teenage Mutant Ninja Turtles* comic book. That first issue sold for just $1.50, but it's now worth thousands of dollars! The popularity of the characters soon inspired a TV show.

A group of teenagers who loves pizza and hanging out sounds pretty normal, but the Teenage Mutant Ninja Turtles are anything but normal! The four ninja warriors fell into a sewer and were exposed to some gnarly toxic sludge that transformed them from regular turtles into super humanoid turtles. Named after four legendary Renaissance artists, Leonardo, Donatello, Raphael, and Michelangelo are out to save the world from evil. Their sensei Yoshi, aka Splinter, raised the four turtles like sons, and taught them everything they know about martial arts. Splinter, a humanoid rat, was also exposed to the same toxic sludge. The martial-arts master has a lifelong feud with Shredder, who is determined to destroy him. The Turtles often team up with Channel 6 news reporter April O'Neill as they battle Shredder and other villains, including Krang, a disembodied brain from Dimension X who wants to take over the world.

The show inspired several films, including the two recent hits starring Megan Fox. A new generation is discovering what many already know about *TMNT*. These four turtles aren't just fearless ninja warriors, they're pretty funny guys too. Cowabunga! Let's kick some shell!

STARRING:
Cam Clarke, Townsend Coleman, Barry Gordon, and Rob Paulsen

NETWORK:
CBS

DID YOU KNOW?
The TMNT inspired a live musical tour, called Coming Out of Their Shells. The musical was sponsored by Pizza Hut—of course!

Saw it! ☐   Rating: ☆☆☆☆☆
Date: ___ / ___ / _____   With: _____
Notes: _____
_____

68

THE POWERPUFF GIRLS

GENRE:
Animated Adventure

AGE:
8+

SEASONS:
6

STARRING:
Cathy Cavadini,
Elizabeth Daily,
and
Tara Strong

By combining sugar, spice, and everything nice, Professor Utonium thought he was concocting three perfect little girls. But somehow a little Chemical X got added to the mix, creating the Powerpuff Girls: Blossom, Bubbles, and Buttercup.

With superpowers that help them save Townsville from evil, the Powerpuff Girls often face off against supervillain monkey Mojo Jojo, who is always scheming to take over the world or destroy the Powerpuff Girls. Blossom, the pink leader of the Powerpuff Girls, uses her smarts and element of "everything nice" to outwit enemies. Bubbles, the blue-loving sweetheart, uses her element of sugar, of course. Buttercup, who's signature color is green, uses her element of spice to fight any foe.

Whether they're confronting a zombie magician, mixing it up with the Gangreen Gang, or accidentally creating a monster, Blossom, Bubbles, and Buttercup prove girls can be strong and feminine at the same time, fighting crime with style, class, and their signature Powerpuff flair!

DID YOU KNOW?

The Powerpuffs are known by different names around the world. In Italy, they are called Lolly, Dolly, and Molly. In Latin America they're known as Bombón, Burbuja, and Bellota (or Chocolate, Bubble, and Acorn).

Saw it! ☐ Rating: ☆☆☆☆☆
Date: ___/___/_____ With: _____
Notes: _____
_____

DEXTER'S LABORATORY

Dexter is a boy-genius with a secret lab in his house, where he invents all kinds of super cool stuff. He's always trying to keep big sister Dee Dee out of his lab, and competes with his equally genius next-door neighbor, Mandark, who has his own much larger at-home lab.

As a serious scientist, Dexter is constantly creating new experiments and inventions that create havoc. Whether he's traveling back in time to understand the origin of fire, transforming his sister into a giant or a monster, or making a "mom-droid" robot to take over for his sick mom, Dexter's ridiculously smart brain is constantly coming up with new ideas. But even though this kid is a genius, he's a lot like every other kid—he would love to keep his sister out of his room, avoid detention, and when he can, save planet Earth from a horrifyingly destructive meteor storm.

When he's not saving the world, Dexter likes going to his favorite restaurant, Burrito Palace; throwing snowballs with his dad; and of course, trying to outsmart Mandark. Dexter is totally relatable and fun to watch, with clever dialogue, great animation, and zingy jokes. You'll love this modern classic cartoon!

DID YOU KNOW?

Dexter has an accent because, as creator Genndy Tartakovsky has said, "all well-known scientists have accents!"

GENRE:
Animated
Adventure

AGE:
7+

SEASONS:
5

STARRING:
Christine
Cavanaugh,
Kath Soucie,
and
Jeff Bennett

Saw it! ☐ Rating: ☆☆☆☆☆

Date: ___ / ___ / _____ With: _____

Notes: _____

_____

THE SMURFS

GENRE:
Animated
Adventure

AGE:
4+

SEASONS:
9

MADE BY:
Peyo

"Now, now! We all need to smurf down!"
—Brainy Smurf

Originally based on a Belgian comic strip by artist Peyo, *The Smurfs* became a TV series in 1981 and quickly rose to international fame. With their tiny mushroom houses, blue skin, white hats, and special Smurf language, the smurfs are "smurftastic!"

There are a bunch of smurfs who live in Smurf Village. Many have an adjective as their first name, such as Grouchy Smurf, Brainy Smurf, Clumsy Smurf, and Lazy Smurf. Others have a job as their first name, such as Actor Smurf or Farmer Smurf. While most Smurfs are boys, there is one girl amongst them: the beautiful blonde Smurfette. There's also Papa Smurf, a 543-year-old Smurf who takes care of everyone in Smurf Village with a magical touch. Evil wizard Gargamel is always trying to catch the smurfs for devious purposes, such as turning them into gold. Gargamel's mischievous cat, Azrael, is often lurking nearby too. When the Smurfs aren't trying to escape from danger, they celebrate being Smurfs with Olympic-style Smurfic Games!

The Smurfs are always getting into trouble, and their silly adventures are fun to watch. For a smurfing good time, you should definitely smurf over to your screen and watch *The Smurfs*!

STARRING:
Don Messick,
Lucille Bliss, and
Paul Winchell

NETWORK:
NBC

SPIN-OFFS
The Smurfs Movie
The Smurfs 2

DID YOU KNOW?
The Smurf language uses the word *smurf* in place of nouns, verbs, and adjectives. So have yourself a smurftastic smurf!

Saw it! ☐   Rating: ☆☆☆☆☆

Date: ___/___/_____ With: _____

Notes: _____

_____

71

ADVENTURE TIME

GENRE:
Animated
Adventure

AGE:
10+

SEASONS:
7 and counting

MADE BY:
Pendleton
Ward

*"What time is it?
Adventure time!"*
—Finn

DID YOU KNOW?
Each episode takes about four months to animate; the animation is done in South Korea, and then the episode comes back to the United States for review before it airs.

In a strange and magical world, Finn and Jake, a boy and his best friend (who happens to be a dog that can change his appearance), protect The Land of Ooo. In their many amazing adventures, they encounter Princess Bubblegum, The Ice King, Marceline the Vampire Queen, and even a Lumpy Space Princess.

Through their adventures, such as tracking down the Gut Grinder, helping Donny the grass ogre (who's kind of obnoxious), and trying to get the Crystal Eye out of a dank dungeon, Finn and Jake encounter incredible creatures and places—from a phantom called the Fear Feaster to a robot who throws pies. Lady Rainicorn, a rainbow-bellied unicorn who speaks Korean, is a fan favorite. Finn and Jake even travel into the belly of a monster to save someone, only to discover a party of bears inside. Unlike most cartoon characters, Finn ages with each season, so viewers can watch him grow and change.

This animated world may be a bit strange, but *Adventure Time* has been praised by critics for its imaginative storytelling, unique humor, and delightful dialogue. This is a show that's adored by kids, teens, and adults alike.

Creator Pendleton Ward has said the show was inspired by the uber-popular fantasy role-playing game Dungeons & Dragons. It started out as a 7-minute film that quickly went viral. After several years, the series has won a ton of awards, including Emmys, Annies, Kids' Choice and Teen Choice awards, and there's even been talk of a future feature film!

STARRING:
Jeremy Shada
and
John DiMaggio

NETWORK:
Cartoon
Network

Saw it! ☐ Rating: ☆☆☆☆☆
Date: ___ / ___ / _____ With: _____
Notes: _____
_____

72

THE GUMBY SHOW

GENRE:
Animated
Adventure

AGE:
4+

SEASONS:
Hundreds
of episodes
created over
40 years

MADE BY:
Art Clokey

"If you've got
a heart, then
Gumby's a part
of you."
— From the
classic theme

The Gumby Show was the very first Claymation show on TV. It first aired in the 1950s and 1960s and then returned in the 1980s. Starring a bendy green boy named Gumby and his orange horse Pokey, Gumby is tremendously low-tech—which is exactly what makes it worth watching. The show turns shape-shifting clay into art in motion and stimulates the imagination. Gumby's creator, Art Clokey, was a pioneer in Claymation, the process of carefully moving and taking thousands of photographs of clay figures to create an animated movie or TV show. The craftsmanship on Gumby lead to Bob the Builder, Shaun the Sheep, Wallace and Gromit, and loads of other shows.

Despite being stretchy, green, and cut from a slab of clay, Gumby is an average boy with parents, friends, and a few enemies—the notorious Blockheads. Gumby even plays in a band called The Clayboys. But it's hard to ignore what makes him unique. Gumby can stretch himself tall or flatten himself out whenever he needs. Cooler still, he and Pokey can walk in and out of books and get in on the action. In each episode they embark on weird adventures and learn all kinds of important life lessons. Throughout the series, Gumby models everyday heroism in big and small ways. Viewers will find enjoying this show isn't a stretch. In fact, most people don't just say they like Gumby, they say they love him!

SPIN-OFFS

Gumby Adventures
Gumby: The Movie

STARRING:
Dal McKennon,
Norma
MacMillan,
Bobby
Nicholson,
and
Art Clokey

NETWORK:
NBC

DID YOU KNOW?
Art Clokey's father, who had a large cowlick in his hair, inspired Gumby's appearance.

Saw it! ☐   Rating: ☆☆☆☆☆
Date: ___ / ___ / _____   With: _____
Notes: _____
_____

73

THE SIMPSONS

GENRE:
Animated
Comedy

AGE:
12+

SEASONS:
27 and counting

MADE BY:
Matt Groening

"Ay, caramba!"
—Bart Simpson

You could watch a different episode of *The Simpsons* every week for 10 years and never get bored! This animated family sitcom has fart gags, absurdist humor, and cartoon slapstick right alongside political humor, social satire, and high-brow cultural references. The show ushered in the trend of creating cartoons for adults, but *The Simpsons* is loved by all ages, and it's miles above the rest in originality and quality of its writing.

Created by Matt Groening in 1987, the yellow-skinned Simpsons never age. Each week they face similar problems; Parents Homer and Marge deal with marriage, home, and money problems, while their children, Bart, Lisa, and Maggie, deal with sibling rivalry, crushes, detention, and grades. Many of the crises are caused by Homer, who is a lovable but lazy, irresponsible, and unreasonable family man. Like a dog, Homer is loyal, devoted, and loving— but lacks common sense or impulse control. Marge, with her bright blue beehive hairdo, tries to manage the chaos but sometimes loses her temper. 10-year-old Bart is an impish troublemaker; 8-year-old Lisa is a precocious, politically correct, straight-A student; and after 30 years, 1-year-old Maggie is still crawling and sucking her pacifier. The family may seem dysfunctional, but don't have a cow, man! Underneath the antics, *The Simpsons* shines with strong family values.

STARRING:
Dan Castellaneta,
Julie Kavner,
Nancy Cartwright,
Yeardley Smith,
Harry Shearer,
and
Hank Azaria

NETWORK:
Fox

SPIN-OFFS

Futurama
The Simpsons Movie

DID YOU KNOW?

Doh! Homer's utterance of surprised disappointment is now listed in the *Oxford English Dictionary*.

Saw it! ☐   Rating: ☆☆☆☆☆

Date: ___ / ___ / _____   With: _____

Notes: _____

_____

74

SHAUN THE SHEEP

GENRE:
Animated
Comedy

AGE:
5+

SEASONS:
4

STARRING:
John Sparkes,
Justin Fletcher,
Richard Webber,
Kate Harbour,
and
Jo Allen

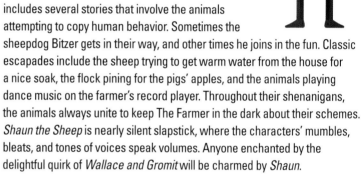

From Aardman Animations, the awesome folks who created *Wallace and Gromit, Shaun the Sheep* is a Claymation masterpiece. In this charming series, Shaun is the chief sheep at Mossy Bottom Farm in northern England. He's the sharpest sheep in the flock, so he tends to hatch plots, draw diagrams, and call the shots. Shaun and his flock are particularly captivated by human activities and the gadgets and gizmos they use to enjoy life on the farm. Each 7-minute episode includes several stories that involve the animals attempting to copy human behavior. Sometimes the sheepdog Bitzer gets in their way, and other times he joins in the fun. Classic escapades include the sheep trying to get warm water from the house for a nice soak, the flock pining for the pigs' apples, and the animals playing dance music on the farmer's record player. Throughout their shenanigans, the animals always unite to keep The Farmer in the dark about their schemes. *Shaun the Sheep* is nearly silent slapstick, where the characters' mumbles, bleats, and tones of voices speak volumes. Anyone enchanted by the delightful quirk of *Wallace and Gromit* will be charmed by *Shaun*.

SPIN-OFFS
Shaun the Sheep Movie

DID YOU KNOW?
Claymation is a painstaking process. *Shaun the Sheep* animators produce just two to three minutes of footage every week.

Saw it! ☐ Rating: ☆☆☆☆☆
Date: ___/___/_____ With: _____
Notes: _____

THE NEW TOM AND JERRY SHOW

Tom and Jerry started as theatrical short films, winning seven Academy Awards for Animated Short Film. But the films that won all those awards never made it to TV. When the cartoons first aired in 1965, they were in a heavily edited and toned-down form. The efforts of Tom the cat to catch Jerry the mouse represent some of the most violent humor in theatrical animation. There are plots involving hammers and firecrackers. Tom and Jerry even whack each other with baseball bats, brooms, and bricks.

Tom and Jerry's battles all but vanished in the kinder, gentler 1970s. In *The New Tom and Jerry Show*, which premiered in 1975, Tom and Jerry are best friends who work together to fight villains and solve mysteries. This classic cat-and-mouse duo surely belongs in the Cartoon Hall of Fame.

DID YOU KNOW?

The Simpsons' show-within-a-show, *The Itchy and Scratchy Show*, is a parody of *Tom and Jerry.*

GENRE:
Animated Comedy

AGE:
5+

SEASONS:
1

SPIN-OFFS

The Tom and Jerry Show
The Tom and Jerry Comedy Show
Tom and Jerry Kids

STARRING:
Henry Corden,
Kathy Gori,
Don Messick,
Alan Oppenheimer,
Joe E. Ross,
and
Hal Smith

Saw it! ☐   Rating: ☆☆☆☆☆
Date: ___/___/_____ With: _____
Notes: _____

76

THE FLINTSTONES

GENRE:
Animated
Comedy

AGE:
5+

SEASONS:
6

MADE BY:
William Hanna
and Joseph
Barbera

"Yabbadabba-
doo!"
—Fred
Flintstone

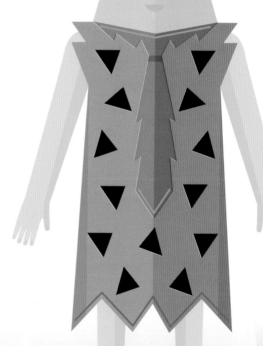

A 1960s cartoon about a prehistoric family might sound like a perplexing premise for a show, but the unique concept hit the funny bones of kids and adults alike. Inspired by *The Honeymooners*, the hugely popular sitcom from the 1950s, *The Flintstones* was TV's first primetime, animated sitcom. Like Ralph Kramden of *The Honeymooners*, Fred Flintstone is an average working-class man who is quick to holler at his wife, Wilma, and his loyal best friend Barney Rubble. The Flintstones have a pet dinosaur named Dino and a baby named Pebbles. The Rubbles, their neighbors, have a son named Bamm-Bamm.

The best jokes are the crazy gadgets, appliances, tools, and cars the residents of Bedrock use each day. A shower is a woolly mammoth spraying water from its trunk, and a laundry machine is a pelican with a throat full of sudsy water. Birds with long beaks serve as hedge clippers, record-player needles, and even the inner mechanics of a camera. These animals often make disgruntled one-liners about their jobs as appliances or tools.

Fred is grouchy when he punches in as brontocrane operator at the Slate Rock and Gravel Company, but when he finishes another day and comes home to his family—or bowls a strike—he does a happy dance that's prehistorically adorable! Watch a few episodes, and you too will be cheering "Yabbadabba-doo!"

STARRING:
Alan Reed,
Jean Vander Pyl,
Mel Blanc, and
Bea Benaderet

NETWORK:
ABC

SPIN-OFFS

The Man Called Flintstone
The Pebbles and Bamm-Bamm Show
The Flintstones
The Flintstones in Viva Rock Vegas

DID YOU KNOW?

The cereals Fruity Pebbles and Cocoa Pebbles are named after The Flintstone's baby daughter, Pebbles.

Saw it! ☐   Rating: ☆☆☆☆☆
Date: ___/___/_____   With: _____
Notes: _____

77

SPONGEBOB SQUAREPANTS

GENRE:
Animated
Comedy

AGE:
6+

SEASONS:
10 and counting

STARRING:
Tom Kenny,
Bill Fagerbakke,
Rodger
Bumpass,
Clancy Brown,
Carolyn
Lawrence, and
Mr. Lawrence

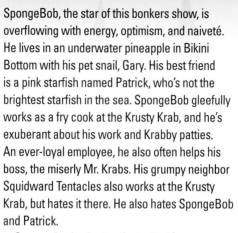

SpongeBob, the star of this bonkers show, is overflowing with energy, optimism, and naiveté. He lives in an underwater pineapple in Bikini Bottom with his pet snail, Gary. His best friend is a pink starfish named Patrick, who's not the brightest starfish in the sea. SpongeBob gleefully works as a fry cook at the Krusty Krab, and he's exuberant about his work and Krabby patties. An ever-loyal employee, he also often helps his boss, the miserly Mr. Krabs. His grumpy neighbor Squidward Tentacles also works at the Krusty Krab, but hates it there. He also hates SpongeBob and Patrick.

Some episodes feature fantastical story lines; in one episode Squidward gets stuck in a freezer for 2,000 years and travels through time. Sometimes the plots are more ordinary; in another episode Patrick invents a board game and wants his friends to play. In many episodes, Plankton, the dastardly owner of The Chum Bucket, a second-rate seafood restaurant, schemes to steal the secret recipe for Krabby patties. Blending all these elements together into an underwater brew of creativity, this kooky show somehow manages to be both sincere and satiric, as well as innocent and weird.

DID YOU KNOW?
Stephen Hillenburg, the creator of the show, used to be a marine biologist.

SPIN-OFFS
The SpongeBob SquarePants Movie
The SpongeBob Movie: Sponge Out of Water

Saw it! ☐ Rating: ☆☆☆☆☆
Date: ___/___/_____ With: _____
Notes: _____

THE BUGS BUNNY SHOW

78

Chomping confidently on a carrot with ears held high, Bugs Bunny is more than a TV character. He's an institution, and his silly spirit pervades popular culture.

In this entertaining series, Bugs Bunny presents three new cartoons in each episode. He also "educates" audiences with silly facts about animals and humans. The cartoons feature characters like Sylvester Cat, Tweety Bird, Daffy Duck, Porky Pig, Road Runner and Wile E. Coyote, Speedy Gonzales, and of course, Bugs Bunny. Each of the animated critters has their own silly personality. Elmer Fudd has been 'hunting wabbits' for 85 years. Bugs Bunny always outsmarts him—and usually humiliates him. Likewise, the Road Runner always evades his predator, Wile E. Coyote. Together, the gang throws themselves into the slapstick comedy they're known for.

The Bugs Bunny Show's hijinks appeal to both young and old. This show is a classic with timeless comedy and sophisticated concepts. Plus puddy tats, wascawwy wabbits, and a pantless pig!

GENRE:
Animated Comedy

AGE:
7+

SEASONS:
3

SPIN-OFFS

The Bugs Bunny/ Road Runner Hour
The Bugs Bunny/Looney Tunes Comedy Hour
The Looney Tunes Show
Baby Looney Tunes

DID YOU KNOW?
Tweety, the cute yellow bird, was originally pink—and named Orson!

STARRING:
Mel Blanc,
June Foray,
Stan Freberg,
Hal Smith,
and
Daws Butler

Saw it! ☐ Rating: ☆☆☆☆☆
Date: ___/___/_____ With: _____
Notes: _____
_____

79

ANIMANIACS

GENRE:
Animated
Comedy

AGE:
7+

SEASONS:
5

MADE BY:
Tom Ruegger

*"We protest you calling us 'little kids.'
We prefer to be called 'vertically-
impaired pre-adults.'"*
—Yakko

What happens when a bunch of animated characters are too zany for regular cartoons? Meet the Animaniacs: a group of characters that bring a bunch of silly, mischievous fun to each and every episode.

Executive produced by Hollywood superstar Steven Spielberg, *Animaniacs* is an animated variety show, where each episode features skits with different characters. There's Yakko, Dot, and Wakko Warner, who have been locked away in the Warner Bros. water tower until now. Pinky and the Brain are mice that are always plotting world domination. Pesto, Squit, and Bobby make up the Goodfeathers, a team of New York pigeons who obsess over Martin Scorsese. Rita and Runt, a cat and dog that like to sing, just want to find a good, loving home.

With its irreverent humor, clever catchphrases, and smart recurring gags, the *Animaniacs* is a barrel of laughs. References to Hollywood movies and parodies of popular shows, such as *Power Rangers* and *Friends*, make the show appealing to both kids and adults. With so many characters in the *Animaniacs* gang, there's an endless array of possibilities to entertain you each season. Whether you're watching the Warners spend the night in Dracula's Transylvanian castle or admiring Pinky and Brain's use of Merlin's book of magic to take over the world, you're bound to enjoy the wacky antics of *Animaniacs*!

STARRING:
Rob Paulsen,
Tress MacNeille,
and
Jess Harnell

NETWORK:
Fox Kids,
The WB

DID YOU KNOW?
Kooky, crazy Wakko, Yakko, and Dot are based on creator Tom Ruegger's three kids!

Saw it! ☐ Rating: ☆☆☆☆☆
Date: ___/ ___/ _____ With: _____
Notes: _____
_____

80

HEY ARNOLD!

GENRE:
Animated
Comedy

AGE:
7+

SEASONS:
5

STARRING:
Lane Toran,
Spencer Klein,
Jamil
Walker Smith,
and
Francesca
Marie Smith

Hey Arnold! is all about 9-year-old Arnold, who lives at the Sunset Arms boarding house in the inner city with his somewhat eccentric grandparents, Pookie and Phil, and an assortment of other entertaining characters. He has some good friends too, including Helga (who has a huge crush on him) and Gerald, a cool kid with street smarts and a vast knowledge of urban legends.

Arnold encounters a bunch of other kids in his day-to-day adventures in the fourth grade, including Rhonda, a popular fashion diva; Phoebe, the smartest girl in school; and Eugene, everyone's favorite geek. There are some kids that give Arnold trouble too, like bully Harold and his sidekicks, Stinky and Sid. In each episode, Arnold learns valuable lessons from his teachers, friends, or the other residents in the boarding house.

The city of Hillwood, where Arnold lives, is a mash-up of Seattle, Portland, and Brooklyn. With its nods to jazz and opera, and references to famous poets, such as Walt Whitman and William Carlos Williams, *Hey Arnold!* has expanded viewers' appreciation for the arts. The show has been praised for its portrayal of diversity and inner-city life, and quickly became a cult classic after its debut in 1994.

DID YOU KNOW?

Creator Craig Bartlett originally created Arnold as a Claymation character while working on *Pee-wee's Playhouse.*

Saw it! ☐   Rating: ☆☆☆☆☆
Date: ___/ ___/ _____ With: _____
Notes: _____
_____

THE ROCKY & BULLWINKLE SHOW

Welcome to *The Rocky & Bullwinkle Show*, an entertaining mash up that's part variety show, part classic cartoon, and part satire. Over the seasons, this series was known by a few different names, including *Rocky and His Friends* and *The Bullwinkle Show.*

The main characters are Rocky, a flying squirrel, and Bullwinkle, a fairly dimwitted moose. Each episode features their run-ins with Boris and Natasha, two Russian spies that can't be trusted. Unlike other cartoons, there are weekly cliffhangers. The furry friends' first adventure spans 40 episodes, as Boris and Natasha plot to uncover the missing ingredient in their jet-fuel formula.

Episodes also include fractured fairy tales and poetry, all narrated by a moose. One delightful segment follows Mr. Peabody and Sherman, a genius dog and his boy. With satirical jokes aplenty and imaginative segments, *The Rocky & Bullwinkle Show* still shines today as a slyly sophisticated gem.

SPIN-OFFS

Boris and Natasha: The Movie
Dudley Do-Right
The Adventures of Rocky & Bullwinkle Movie
Mr. Peabody & Sherman
The Mr. Peabody & Sherman Show

DID YOU KNOW?

Boris and Natasha were inspired by the husband and wife in Charles Addams' *New Yorker* cartoons—the same characters that inspired Gomez and Morticia Addams of *The Addams Family!*

GENRE:
Animated Comedy

AGE:
8+

SEASONS:
5

STARRING:
June Foray,
Bill Scott, and
Paul Frees

Saw it! ☐ Rating: ☆☆☆☆☆

Date: ___/___/_____ With: _____

Notes: _____

_____

82

THE JETSONS

GENRE:
Animated
Comedy

AGE:
5+

SEASONS:
3

MADE BY:
William Hanna
and Joseph
Barbera

"Jane! Stop this crazy thing!"
—George Jetson

Just like *The Flintstones*, *The Jetsons* is a 30-minute cartoon about a family and their day-to-day life. But this show is set far in the future. George Jetson, his wife Jane, daughter Judy, and son Elroy live in Orbit City, and just like *The Flintstones*, all the novel gizmos, architecture, and futuristic technology make the show memorable.

The buildings float high in the sky, and characters travel from structure to structure in glass aerocars. George's aerocar converts into his briefcase, which is just one of the many nifty visual wonders the show offers. Futuristic conveniences and time-saving devices, such as Rosie the Robot, who cleans the Jetsons' Skypad and brings a bit of sass to each episode, plus jet packs and dinners that appear at the push of a button, help create a utopian futurescape. Precursors to smart watches and video chatting are also part of this world. Episodes involve George getting lost on the moon or volunteering to test a new invention that shrinks him down to just six inches. In other episodes, Judy meets her teen idol, Jane enters a beauty pageant, and the family adopts their talking dog Astro.

It isn't the most accurate depiction of the future, but the show has inspired real-life fashion, movies, and more. Watching this show is the most fun way to travel to the past and the future all at once!

STARRING:
George O'Hanlon, Penny Singleton, Janet Waldo, Daws Butler, and Mel Blanc

NETWORK:
ABC

SPIN-OFFS

The Jetsons Meet the Flintstones
Rockin' with Judy Jetson

DID YOU KNOW?
The Jetsons was ABC's first show to be broadcast in color.

Saw it! ☐   Rating: ☆☆☆☆☆
Date: ___ / ___ / _____   With: _____
Notes: _____
_____

83

UGLY BETTY

GENRE:
Comedy

AGE:
13+

SEASONS:
4

STARRING:
America Ferrera

Adapted from a Colombian soap opera, *Ugly Betty* follows a kind, smart 22-year-old girl from Queens who lands a job in Manhattan. But since she wears unflattering clothes and has frizzy bangs, bushy eyebrows, and braces, she doesn't quite fit in with everyone else who works at *Mode*, a high-fashion magazine.

The series shines with over-the-top, soap-opera-style drama that is both funny and absorbing. Early in the series, Betty makes all kinds of clumsy missteps and is often the butt of snide commentary from catty co-workers Mark and Amanda. Fortunately, Betty has a close-knit, supportive family at home, where the show's core values of love and inner beauty are shown. Betty eventually wins over some of the coldest hearts at work. While there are some adult themes, the drama never overshadows the comic hijinks, sarcastic one-liners, and quirky characters that make this series a winner.

DID YOU KNOW?

America Ferrera, the actress who played Betty, was also in the movie adaptation of *The Sisterhood of the Traveling Pants*. Producers gave a nod to her work by placing a copy of the book on Betty's nightstand.

Saw it! ☐   Rating: ☆☆☆☆☆
Date: ___ / ___ / _____   With: _____
Notes: _____
_____

MR. BEAN

Mr. Bean is a British comedy that aired from 1992 to 1995. Created by Rowan Atkinson and Richard Curtis, the show stars Atkinson as a comically immature, socially awkward, clueless, all-around weirdo. Atkinson described his character as "a child in a grown man's body." He could also be described as selfish and annoying. Bean goes through his days making a mess of things, breaking things, and irritating people. He has zero sense of personal space. But in Atkinson's talented hands, Mr. Bean isn't just annoying, he's hilarious.

This 1990s show is a throwback to the simple slapstick comedy of *The Carol Burnett Show*, and even Charlie Chaplin. Most impressive is that the show is almost entirely wordless. While there is some dialogue, Atkinson keeps viewers entertained with an extraordinary range of facial expressions and physical antics. There are a few other characters for him to interact with, but they are mostly strangers who are inconvenienced and bothered by Mr. Bean's behavior. Bean can wreak havoc on himself in the simplest situations, including changing into a swimsuit, losing a shoe, or trying to make his TV work. But from the safe distance of your couch, Mr. Bean makes the world a happier, funnier place to be!

GENRE:
Comedy

AGE:
10+

SEASONS:
4

STARRING:
Rowan Atkinson

DID YOU KNOW?

The opening sequence shows Bean descending to Earth as a choir sings, "Ecce homo qui est faba" dramatically. But the translation isn't quite so dramatic. It means, "Behold the man who is a bean."

Saw it! ☐ Rating: ☆☆☆☆☆
Date: ___ / ___ / _____ With: _____
Notes: _____
_____

85

MONTY PYTHON'S FLYING CIRCUS

GENRE:
Comedy

AGE:
14+

SEASONS:
4

MADE BY:
Graham
Chapman,
John Cleese,
Terry Gilliam,
Eric Idle,
Terry Jones, and
Michael Palin

"Nobody expects the Spanish Inquisition!" —An absurd line from a Monty Python sketch that led to many more sketches and memes

DID YOU KNOW?

Anyone applying for British citizenship will want to spend hours watching *Monty Python*. The citizenship exam includes questions about Shakespeare, Stonehenge—and British classic *Monty Python*!

The creators considered naming the show everything from *Owl Stretching Time* to *Bunn, Wackett, Buzzard, Stubble and Boot*, which doesn't make any more sense than *Monty Python's Flying Circus*. And when it finally aired, the show was almost canceled after just one episode. But thankfully this classic comedy survived. The production values are humble, the camera work is a bit shoddy, and by today's standards, the program seems a tad amateurish, but for obsessed fans, sharing *Monty Python* with the next generation is a no-brainer. This British sketch comedy is recommended for anyone who has an outlandish, offbeat sense of humor and an appreciation for comedic anarchy.

With less structure and sillier jokes than Monty Python movies that came later, *The Flying Circus* is chaos. The highly educated writers and performers of the Monty Python troupe are as comfortable making jokes about deep thinkers like Marcel Proust and Karl Marx as they are dressing up as frumpy housewives. The comedy is absurd, sometimes surreal, and always ludicrous. Episodes are a mix of loopy skits, fanciful animation, cheeky humor, and songs. Nonsensical sketches often make use of stock footage, ridiculous accents, and a preposterous set up like a clinic where customers can pay for a 30-minute argument, a hospital for patients suffering from severe over-acting, a class for "self-defense against fresh fruit" and of course, a government agency called the Ministry of Silly Walks. When it comes to Monty Python, no one expects the Spanish Inquisition, but they can always expect to laugh.

STARRING:
Graham Chapman,
John Cleese,
Terry Gilliam,
Eric Idle,
Terry Jones, and
Michael Palin

NETWORK:
BBC, PBS

SPIN-OFFS
And Now for Something Completely Different
Monty Python and the Holy Grail
Life of Brian
The Meaning of Life

Saw it! ☐ Rating: ☆☆☆☆☆
Date: ___ / ___ / _____ With: _____
Notes: _____
_____

86

PEE-WEE'S PLAYHOUSE

GENRE:
Comedy

AGE:
6+

SEASONS:
5

MADE BY:
Paul Reubens

"I know you are,
but what am I?"
—Pee-wee

ee-wee's Playhouse, originally created for a stage act in 80, features Paul Reubens' giddy, childlike character Pee-Vee Herman. He spends his day playing in a gorgeously conceived fantasy ayhouse that would make any child happy. The set is bursting with color, ys, friends, and inanimate objects that surprise and dazzle. There's a talking indow (Mr. Window) and a talking chair (Chairy), along with Globey, Clocky, d Conky the robot—the brain of the show. There are both human characters d puppets, as well as animated sequences. Friends also stop by all the time. ome of the show's regulars are Captain Carl and Cowboy Curtis, retro versions f a cowboy and a sea captain. Another recurring character is Jambi the Genie, blue headed genie that grants wishes and lives in a jeweled box.

Throughout the show's run, Reubens had complete creative control. He also ent much of his own money to make the show a success. With a retro-ntage vibe inspired by Reubens' childhood vorite shows, _The Howdy Doody Show_ and _aptain Kangaroo,_ every episode is about aving fun. With a diverse group of actors and its ender-neutral approach, this show is a big, loud, olorful celebration of individuality!

STARRING:
Paul Reubens,
George McGrath,
and
Alison Mork

NETWORK:
CBS

DID YOU KNOW?

Paul Reubens auditioned to join the cast of _Saturday Night Live_ but didn't make the cut. Thankfully that didn't stop him from sharing his delightful humor with the world!

PIN-OFFS

ee-wee's Big Adventure
ig Top Pee-wee
ee-wee's Playhouse: The Movie
he Pee-wee Herman Story
he Pee-wee Herman Show revival
ee-wee's Big Holiday

Saw it! ☐ Rating: ☆☆☆☆☆
Date: ___/ ___/ _____ With: _____
Notes: _____
_____

87

THE MONKEES

GENRE:
Comedy

AGE:
7+

SEASONS:
2

STARRING:
Davy Jones,
Micky Dolenz,
Michael
Nesmith, and
Peter Tork

"Hey, hey, we're the Monkees!" This catchy line launched every episode of the popular 1960s show. Shortly after the Beatles made their big-screen, musical comedies *A Hard Day's Night* and *Help!*, The Monkees arrived. The band name alludes to another popular animal, and there's a dashing, shaggy-haired Brit to front the band, just like Paul McCartney in the Beatles. But in some ways the fictitious band is closer to *The Partridge Family*, with their real hit songs. The show charts the aspiring rock stars' madcap career and their fun-loving, freewheeling spirits. Their sound was a cross between The Beach Boys and—you guessed it—the Beatles.

While some of the episodes focus on their music and encounters with producers, publicists, and showbiz personnel, there are tons of zany stories too: The Monkees spend a night in a haunted house, The Monkees get stranded in a ghost town, and The Monkees have to hide a horse from their landlord. The show opens with the foursome fooling around, wearing crazy costumes, playing on the beach, and singing their famous song, "Hey, Hey, We're The Monkees." Other infectious hits include, "I'm a Believer" and "Last Train to Clarksville." Are you ready for a little Monkeemania?

SPIN-OFFS
New Monkees

Saw it! ☐ Rating: ☆☆☆☆☆
Date: ___/___/_____ With: _____
Notes: _____
_____

GIDGET

Surf's up, dudes! Gidget is a sassy teenage surfer girl who tends to find her way into trouble. She lives with her father, Russell Lawrence, a widower and professor, in sunny Southern California. She spends most of her time either with her best friend, Larue, or surfing at the beach.

When *Gidget* aired in 1965, the show featured a very different female lead than the other shows on television at the time. Gidget, an independent, smart, and lovable girl, isn't afraid to break the rules. And the adventures she goes on are as eccentric as she is—one episode revolves around a tiny frozen alligator! At the end of each episode, she turns to the camera and tells the audience what she learned, but by the next episode, she's ready to throw the rules out the window again!

Gidget may be a little boy-crazy. She's dating Jeff (also known as Moondoggie), but he's away at college, so she's free to flirt with other boys at the beach. Gidget's married older sister, Anne, often tries to offer advice, but it's usually the wise words of their father that reach Gidget the best. This fun, breezy summer show will have you wanting to hang ten at the beach and meet the Great Kahuna!

SPIN-OFFS
The New Gidget

DID YOU KNOW?
Sally Field, who plays Gidget, improvised saying, "Toodles!" at the end of an episode, and it became her catchphrase.

GENRE:
Comedy

AGE:
7+

SEASONS:
1

STARRING:
Sally Field

Saw it! ☐ Rating: ☆☆☆☆☆
Date: ___/___/_____ With: _____
Notes: _____
_____

THE CAROL BURNETT SHOW

GENRE:
Comedy

AGE:
9+

SEASONS:
11

MADE BY:
Bob Banner
and
Joe Hamilton

"I'm so glad we had
this time together
Just to have a laugh
or sing a song.
Seems we just got
started and before
you know it
Comes the time we
have to say, 'So long.'"
—From the classic
theme song

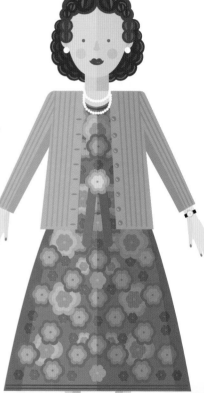

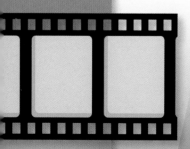

Like Lucille Ball, Carol Burnett is a timeless titan of cockamamie comedy. *The Carol Burnett Show*, which ran from the late 1960s to the late 1970s, is still hilarious 40 years later. It's a one-hour variety show with a huge range of stellar guests, from Ray Charles to Lily Tomlin. Steve Martin even joined the cast of regulars, which included Harvey Korman, Tim Conway, Vicki Lawrence, and Lyle Waggoner, in comic skits and musical numbers. The show featured regular characters, such as Mrs. Wiggins, a silly, incompetent secretary played by Burnett, and an incredibly old geezer played by Conway, who drives everyone crazy by moving so slowly. One of the funniest things about the show is watching the cast crack each other up. Conway would often go out of his way to make Korman laugh, and watching Korman try—and fail—to hold it together is highly entertaining. The show also featured plenty of movie parodies, and even if you don't know the films, the sketches are so wacky, you'll still find yourself laughing. One of the most memorable sketches was a parody of *Gone with the Wind*, in which Burnett as Scarlett O'Hara wears a dress made from window drapes. Sounds resourceful, not silly, right? Consider that she also wore the drape rod as shoulder pads. The result was perfectly preposterous and totally delirious!

SPIN-OFFS

Carol Burnett & Company
Eunice
Mama's Family

STARRING:
Carol Burnett,
Harvey Korman,
Vicki Lawrence,
Lyle Waggoner,
and
Tim Conway

NETWORK:
CBS

DID YOU KNOW?
The first variety show to be led by a woman, *The Carol Burnett Show* won 25 Emmys.

Saw it! ☐ Rating: ☆☆☆☆☆
Date: ___ / ___ / _____ With: _____
Notes: _____
_____

90 THE MICKEY MOUSE CLUB

GENRE:
Comedy

AGE:
2+

SEASONS:
4

MADE BY:
Walt Disney,
Bill Walsh,
and
Hal Adelquist

"Why? Because
we like you!
—Jimmie at the end
of each show, telling
viewers there will
be another episode
tomorrow

ANNETTE

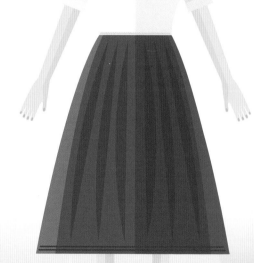

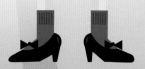

Hey, there! Hi, there! Ho, there! "Who's the leader of the club that's made for you and me?" When you're talking about the *Mickey Mouse Club*, the answer is obvious. M-I-C-K-E-Y M-O-U-S-E!

First airing in 1955, this long-running variety show has entertained multiple generations. The original *Mickey Mouse Club* featured a line-up of teenage Mouseketeers, including Annette Funicello and Tommy Cole. Later the show was revived in full color for new audiences, with stars such as a young Britney Spears and Justin Timberlake.

Walt Disney himself designed the *Mickey Mouse Club* to include cartoons, singing, dancing, comedy, a touch of drama, and a news segment. Monday episodes are all about having fun with music. Tuesday shows feature guest stars. On Wednesdays, anything can happen. Thursdays are circus days. And Friday is a talent round up. At the beginning of each show, the Mouseketeers line up for roll call and introduce themselves. The teenagers are lead by Head Mouseketeer, Jimmie Dodd. He often offers bits of wisdom known as Doddisms and encourages kids to make good choices. Each episode ends with a slower version of the theme song and a promise to "See you real soon!"

Wholesome, precocious, and yet totally relatable, the teenagers feel like best friends. The cast often speaks directly to the camera, inviting viewers to join the jamboree and feel like one of the gang. Watch a few episodes, and soon you'll be longing for your own pair of mouse ears.

SPIN-OFFS
New Mickey Mouse Club
All New Mickey Mouse Club (MMC)

STARRING:
Annette Funicello, Tommy Cole, Jimmie Dodd, and Roy Williams

NETWORK:
Disney, ABC

DID YOU KNOW?
Walt Disney wanted to cast "regular" kids for the show, so he avoided hiring professional actors.

Saw it! ☐ Rating: ☆☆☆☆☆
Date: ___/___/_____ With: _____
Notes: _____
_____

91

THE WIGGLES

GENRE:
Comedy

AGE:
3+

SEASONS:
5

STARRING:
Murray Cook,
Jeff Fatt,
Anthony Field,
and
Greg Page

Did you learn to sing and dance with the Wiggles? If not, you're missing out! The Wiggles, a band from Australia, love to sing, dance, and hang out with their friends Wags the Dog, Dorothy the Dinosaur, Henry the Octopus, and of course, Captain Feathersword.

Since they first started playing together in 1991, The Wiggles have risen to international fame. They've earned many awards, their multi-platinum records are a hit, and they've toured the world. Originally there were just four Wiggles, but as of 2013, some new faces appeared, including the first female Wiggle.

Whether they are trying to wake Jeff up (Everyone yell: WAKE UP, JEFF!), teaching Captain Feathersword to spell, or just riding around in their Big Red Car, The Wiggles are always having fun. Friendship, imagination, and silly, goofy fun are what The Wiggles want to show you, and they have a catchy, colorful way of doing it. So come on, join the dance party and wiggle away!

DID YOU KNOW?
The Wiggles perform for over a million people every year—that's a lot of wiggling!

Saw it! ☐ Rating: ☆☆☆☆☆

Date: ___/___/_____ With: _____

Notes: _____

_____

YOU CAN'T DO THAT ON TELEVISION

You better not say "I don't know" on this show, or else you'll get a giant bucket of slime dumped on your head! You could also get soaked with water or get a pie in the face. There's never a dull moment on *You Can't Do That on Television!*

A variety sketch show featuring young actors, this show has it all: parodies of other TV shows and commercials, silly recurring gags and gimmicks, and a hilarious cast. Each episode is built around a theme, and all the skits go with it, down to the name of the production company listed in the end credits. (The divorce-themed episode was supposedly made by the "Split Down The Middle" production company.) Some sketches are recurring, such as the "opposites" sketch, where everything is opposite; locker jokes, where kids tell jokes from inside their lockers; and of course, the Barth's Burgers sketches where kids eat at a terrible restaurant.

You Can't Do That on Television is packed with slapstick comedy, a talented cast, and a whole lot of slime, which eventually became a hallmark of the Nickelodeon network!

GENRE:
Comedy

AGE:
12+

SEASONS:
10

STARRING:
Les Lye,
Abby Hagyard,
and
Christine
McGlade

DID YOU KNOW?
The green slime is made from a mixture of water, flour, and green gelatin!

Saw it! ☐ Rating: ☆☆☆☆☆
Date: ___ / ___ / _____ With: _____
Notes: _____
_____

93

LITTLE HOUSE ON THE PRAIRIE

GENRE:
Drama

AGE:
7+

SEASONS:
9

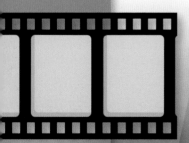

MADE BY:
Based on the books by Laura Ingalls Wilder

DID YOU KNOW?
Little House on the Prairie and *The Waltons* were marketed as family-friendly alternatives to edgier shows like *All In The Family*, *Sanford and Son*, and *Starsky and Hutch*.

" Home is the nicest word there is."
—Laura Ingalls Wilder

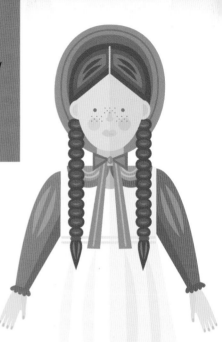

Based on Laura Ingalls Wilder's perennially popular autobiographical books about frontier life, *Little House on the Prairie* is set in the American frontier in the late 19th century. Although the stories were often simplistic and moralizing, the multidimensional acting set this show apart from other shows in the 1970s. (The show was nominated for 16 Emmys!)

STARRING:
Michael Landon,
Melissa Gilbert,
Karen Grassle,
and
Melissa Sue
Anderson

Like the *Little House* novels, the series follows the life of the Ingalls family, told from the point of view of Laura, who is around 6 years old when the series begins. The Ingalls are homesteaders who settle in a quaint home in Walnut Grove, Minnesota. You don't have to be a Laura Ingalls Wilder reader to get hooked on this series. The show immerses viewers in an era of horse-drawn wagons, sleeping bonnets, and schoolhouses with writing tablets. And since the story runs until the Ingalls girls are grown and married, it also features soap-opera-style plotlines. Charles Ingalls, or "Pa," is a farmer and mill worker. Played by Michael Landon, Charles is a strong and compassionate family man. He's an attentive, adoring father and an ideal husband to his wife, Caroline. Their children are Mary, Laura, and Carrie. In later seasons, Grace is born, and three others are adopted. Hard working and self-sufficient, the family has little money, and when the girls start school, they become exposed to wealthier townspeople. One of the original love-to-hate-them characters, Nelly Oleson is a spoiled brat with a snobby mother. Nelly and her mother look down at the Ingalls, who can't afford a lot of things. But the Ingalls show they are truly the richer family. Watch this show and soon you'll agree; the Ingalls may live in a little house, but their hearts are as big as the prairie!

NETWORK:
NBC

SPIN-OFFS

Little House: A New Beginning
Little House on the Prairie: A Look Back to Yesterday

Saw it! ☐ Rating: ☆☆☆☆☆
Date: ___/___/_____ With: _____
Notes: _____
_____

94

DOOGIE HOWSER, M.D.

GENRE:
Drama

AGE:
12+

SEASONS:
4

STARRING:
Neil Patrick
Harris,
Max Casella,
Lisa Dean Ryan,
and
Lawrence
Pressman

Like many other kids, Doogie Howser feels a little out of place, whether he's with adults or other children. But unlike other kids, he's also the world's youngest doctor. *Doogie Howser, M.D.* is a drama about a prodigy who graduated from Princeton when he was 10. Played by a baby-faced Neil Patrick Harris, Doogie lives at home with his parents and follows their rules, but he practices medicine at a hospital where he makes life-saving decisions. The show's sweet mix of comedy and drama is appealing, and viewers can relate to Doogie being someone who doesn't quite fit in.

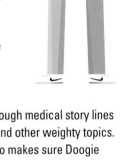

   Doogie can often be found performing surgery, while also worrying about his first kiss or being liked by the popular kids. In one episode, he throws a party when his parents are away so the other kids won't think he's a "freak." Because of his grueling work schedule, Doogie often has to apologize for being late to his on-again/off-again girlfriend Wanda. Life lessons are introduced through medical story lines that touch on AIDS, teen pregnancy, race riots, and other weighty topics. But his goofy, girl-crazy best friend Vinnie Delpino makes sure Doogie never gets too serious.

DID YOU KNOW?
Neil Patrick Harris practiced making stitches on raw chickens.

Saw it! ☐   Rating: ☆☆☆☆☆
Date: ___ / ___ / _____   With: _____
Notes: _____
_____

GILMORE GIRLS

This witty dramedy follows single mother Lorelai Gilmore and her 16-year-old daughter Rory. They are best friends who support each other through changes in jobs, schools, friends, and boyfriends.

The series effortlessly blends family drama with humor and social commentary, as mother and daughter navigate work, school, and dinner at Grandma's house. In the pilot episode, Lorelai asks her parents, Richard and Emily, to help pay for Rory's education at a prestigious private school. They agree to help only if Lorelai and Rory attend formal weekly dinners at their house. The story lines are set against the backdrop of the Gilmores' small hometown, Stars Hollow, Connecticut, where they are surrounded by eccentric characters, such as Lorelai's klutzy best friend, Sookie St. James, and the owner of Luke's Diner, who adds casual humor to the show.

For many fans, the characters' clever dialogue makes the show addictive. Lorelei and Rory are famous for their snarky, rapid-fire banter full of pop-culture references. The series was widely embraced for its feminist role models and quirky depiction of a sisterly mother/daughter relationship.

GENRE:
Drama

AGE:
14+

SEASONS:
7

STARRING:
Lauren Graham,
Alexis Bledel,
Scott Patterson,
Kelly Bishop,
and
Edward
Herrmann

DID YOU KNOW?
The exterior shot of the Dragonfly Inn, where Lorelai works, is the same family home from *The Waltons*.

Saw it! ☐ Rating: ☆☆☆☆☆
Date: ___ / ___ / _____ With: _____
Notes: _____
_____

96

DEGRASSI: THE NEXT GENERATION

GENRE:
Drama

AGE:
14+

SEASONS:
14

MADE BY:
Kit Hood
and
Linda Schuyler

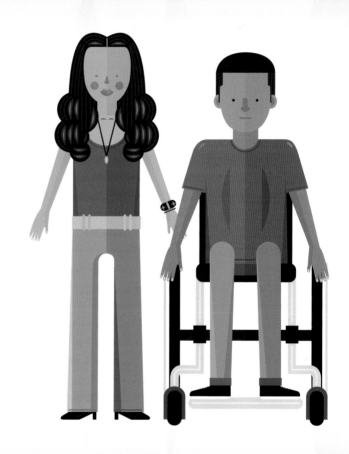

"It's just been one disaster after another after another. That school is cursed." —Ashley

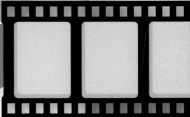

Taking place 14 years after the original show *Degrassi Junior High*, *Degrassi: The Next Generation* brings the drama! From tragedy to scandal, the kids at Degrassi Community School experience it all. While there are definitely moments of lighthearted fun, *Degrassi* features the more serious issues of teenage life, including divorce, teen pregnancy, bullying, eating disorders, and even a school shooting. (Of course, they're also dealing with cliques, crushes, homework, frenemies, team tryouts, and prom.) These very real issues are handled with honesty, care, and empathy. The characters are believable and sympathetic, and it's easy to become invested in their story lines and relationships. Alli struggles to balance her conservative Muslim heritage with her boy-crazy impulses. Jenna learns to find her way as a young mother. And viewers' hearts melt as Adam navigates being a transgender teen. While the cast changes throughout the years as the kids grow up and graduate, *Degrassi* consistently keeps viewers captivated with compelling story lines, insightful dialogue, and talented young actors.

The show launched the careers of several young stars, most notably Aubrey Graham, aka mega recording star Drake, who played Jimmy Brooks. *Degrassi* has won more than 50 awards for writing, directing, and acting. Legions of fans will be pleased to know a new series is in the works on Netflix. Let the *Degrassi* drama continue…

SPIN-OFFS
Degrassi: Next Class

STARRING:
Melinda Shankar,
Aislinn Paul,
A.J. Saudin,
Miriam McDonald,
Shane Kippel,
Stefan Brogren
and
Drake

NETWORK:
CTV,
TeenNick

DID YOU KNOW?
Each episode is named after a song from the 1980s. Totally rad!

Saw it! ☐   Rating: ☆☆☆☆☆
Date: ___/___/_____   With: _____
Notes: _____
_____

97

FREAKS AND GEEKS

GENRE:
Drama

AGE:
14+

SEASONS:
1

MADE BY:
Judd Apatow
and Paul Feig

"Wait a minute.
If I think I'm cool then people will
think I'm cool too? But I already
think I'm cool. But nobody else does."
—Neil Schweiber

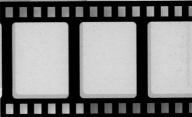

Freaks and Geeks is critically acclaimed and beloved by audiences. Set in the 1980s, each episode features an authentic story line and a stellar cast of young actors who went on to become big stars. As the title suggests, the series follows two groups of high-school students: the freshman "geeks" and the junior and senior "freaks" who are more interested in partying than studying.

The show focuses on Lindsay and Sam Weir. Sam is a ninth-grader who's frequently bullied. His older sister Lindsay is a well-behaved rule follower and an "A" student who starts hanging out with the "freaks." Lindsay must balance her allegiance to school and family with her emerging independence and desire to hang out with the "cool kids." The cool kids include a fresh-faced Seth Rogen as Ken and a young Jason Segel as Nick. Like his older sister, Sam is trying to navigate growing up. He and his friends are socially awkward, obsessed with Steve Martin, devoted to playing Dungeons and Dragons, and determined to figure out where girls fit into their lives.

Unlike their new friends, Lindsay and Sam come from a loving and concerned family, with a nurturing but worried mom and an alarmed dad with a deadpan sense of humor. The show is quirky and a little edgy, but at its core, it's about growing pains and figuring out how to make good choices. The series was inexplicably canceled after one season, which was a true television tragedy for its devoted fans.

STARRING:
Linda Cardellini,
John Francis Daley,
James Franco,
Samm Levine,
Seth Rogen,
Jason Segel,
Martin Starr,
Becky Ann Baker,
Joe Flaherty,
and
Busy Philipps

NETWORK:
NBC

DID YOU KNOW?

Every plot point in *Freaks and Geeks* was based on a real event that happened in the lives of the show's writers.

Saw it! ☐ Rating: ☆☆☆☆☆

Date: ___/___/_____ With: _____

Notes: _____

_____

98

LASSIE

GENRE:
Drama

AGE:
5+

SEASONS:
19

STARRING:
Jon Provost,
June Lockhart,
and
Hugh Reilly

If your dog is your best friend, you know how smart and clever canine pals can be. Over 19 seasons, Lassie and her human family have all types of adventures on their farm. Whether Lassie is tending to motherless baby birds or helping Timmy out of a jam, she's always the hero.

Lassie is an extraordinarily smart, brave, and sensitive collie; it's almost as if she can communicate with her human companions just by barking. In the first few seasons of the show, Lassie is part of the Miller family. Later she is part of the Martin family, and eventually she joins the US Forest Service. In every episode, Lassie either goes to get help when people are in trouble, or jumps in to save them herself if needed.

The show was based on a series of popular movies in the 1940s and early 1950s. Originally, the show was in black and white, but it made the transition to color in 1965. As one of the longest running shows in television history, *Lassie* is not only famous for portraying a really smart dog, but also for telling the story of a farm family with strong values. Of course, this heartwarming classic is worth a watch just to see how Lassie always manages to save the day.

DID YOU KNOW?

In the pilot, Lassie was played by a dog named Pal, but for the rest of the show, Pal's pups, Lassie Junior, Spook, and Baby played Lassie.

Saw it! ☐ Rating: ☆☆☆☆☆
Date: ___/___/_____ With: _____
Notes: _____
_____

THE WALTONS

Told from the viewpoint of adult John-Boy, the oldest of seven siblings, *The Waltons* follows a family living in rural Virginia during the Great Depression and World War II. The Walton family includes Olivia and John (or Ma and Pa), their children, and the grandparents.

In each episode, the family works together to do the right thing, whether they open their home to a stranded traveler, help an orphaned kid learn what a loving and trusting family looks like, or lend a hand in their community. Traditional, wholesome values and lessons are woven throughout every storyline. Money is tight in the Walton home, and the family must come together to support each other and make ends meet. As the seasons roll on, the family experiences a lot together: college, courtships, marriages, career changes, new babies, and even illness and death.

Each episode ends with everyone in the house going to sleep. As the lights go out, everyone says goodnight to each other. Watching *The Waltons* will make you feel like you are a part of their big family, and you'll soon be saying "Goodnight, John-Boy" too!

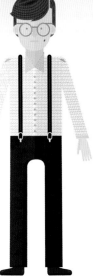

GENRE:
Drama

AGE:
7+

SEASONS:
9

STARRING:
Jon Walmsley,
Mary Beth,
McDonough,
Eric Scott,
Judy Norton,
David W. Harper,
Kami Cotler,
and
Richard Thomas

DID YOU KNOW?

The cast of *The Waltons* consider themselves family and have stayed friends for over 50 years.

Saw it! ☐ Rating: ☆☆☆☆☆
Date: ___ / ___ / _____ With: _____
Notes: _____
_____

100

SHELLEY DUVALL'S FAERIE TALE THEATRE

GENRE:
Drama

AGE:
7+

SEASONS:
6

MADE BY:
Shelley Duvall

Gretel: Why would you want to eat him? Witch: I am going to eat him, because that is what witches like to do!

Some of the most beloved stories have been told over and over for hundreds of years. *Faerie Tale Theatre*, which first aired in 1982, retells some of these classic stories. Shelley Duvall, the actress who has given a variety of quirky performances, including the odd-ball Olive Oyl in the movie version of *Popeye*, created and produced this enchanting anthology of fables.

Duvall enlists renowned directors like Tim Burton and Francis Ford Coppola to contribute to the series. Stars such as Pee-wee Herman and Robin Williams play classic characters like Pinocchio, the frog prince, the princess in *The Princess and the Pea*, witches, sorcerers, and more. While the tales are timeless, this show updates the stories to include more modern, humorous dialogue. For example, the snobbish princess in *The Tale of the Frog Prince* complains about the prince by calling him a "miserable creep " who has the "brains of a shrimp." The cast is also more racially diverse than many of those found on television.

The episodes are clearly staged as a play, and the action takes place on sets with far less razzle dazzle than you may be used to, but the emphasis is on the language and the excellent performances. More than 30 years later, this show still deserves a standing ovation.

SPIN-OFFS
Shelley Duvall's Tall Tales & Legends

STARRING:
Shelley Duvall

NETWORK:
Showtime

DID YOU KNOW?
The series was inspired by *Shirley Temple's Storybook*, a TV series that was popular in the late 1950s and early 1960s.

Saw it! ☐ Rating: ☆☆☆☆☆
Date: ___ / ___ / _____ With: _____
Notes: _____
_____

101

MY SO-CALLED LIFE

GENRE:
Drama

AGE:
14+

SEASONS:
1

STARRING:
Claire Danes,
Jared Leto,
Wilson Cruz,
Devon
Gummersall,
and
A.J. Langer

Canceled after just one season, this 1994 family drama still has a cult following. It's bittersweet, intelligent, and filled with great characters and dialogue. Claire Danes plays 15-year-old Angela. Angela narrates the scenes with a sardonic voiceover that honestly describes the inner turmoil teenagers face. In the show's first episode, she dyes her hair red as she tries to figure out who she is and who she wants to be. She sheds her childhood friends, Brian, the sweet boy next door, and Sharon, a more conventional BFF; becomes part of a less innocent group; and develops a crush on dreamy renegade Jordan Catalano. Her new best friend, Rayanne, is wild, outrageous, and unsupervised by her single mom. Rayanne's other best friend, Rickie, wears eyeliner and bright clothes, and eventually gets kicked out of his house because he's gay.

The show tackles intense subjects like school violence, censorship, homelessness, and more. The show could have been very dark, but with witty, clever writing and authentic, likable characters, instead it's an absolute treasure.

DID YOU KNOW?
The school scenes were filmed at University High School in Los Angeles, where other popular shows such as *Lizzie McGuire*, *7th Heaven,* and *Parenthood* were also filmed.

Saw it! ☐ Rating: ☆☆☆☆☆
Date: ___/ ___/ _____ With: _____
Notes: _____
_____

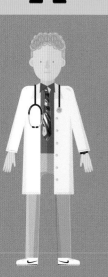

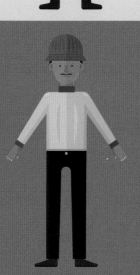

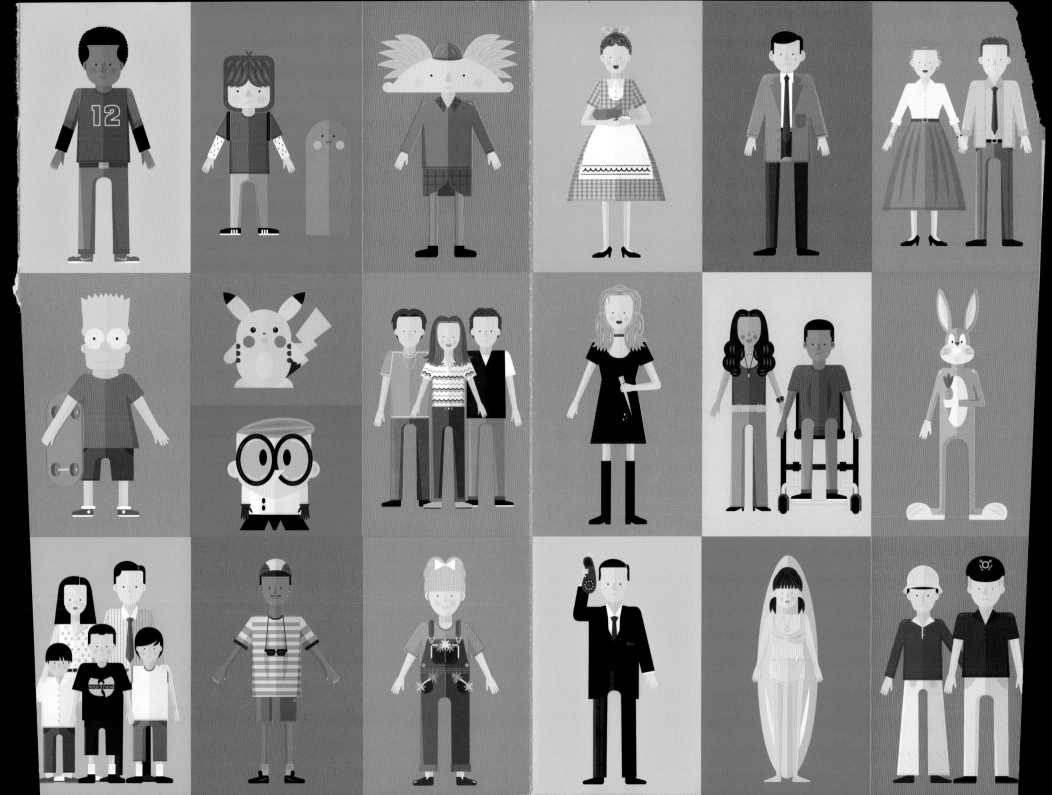

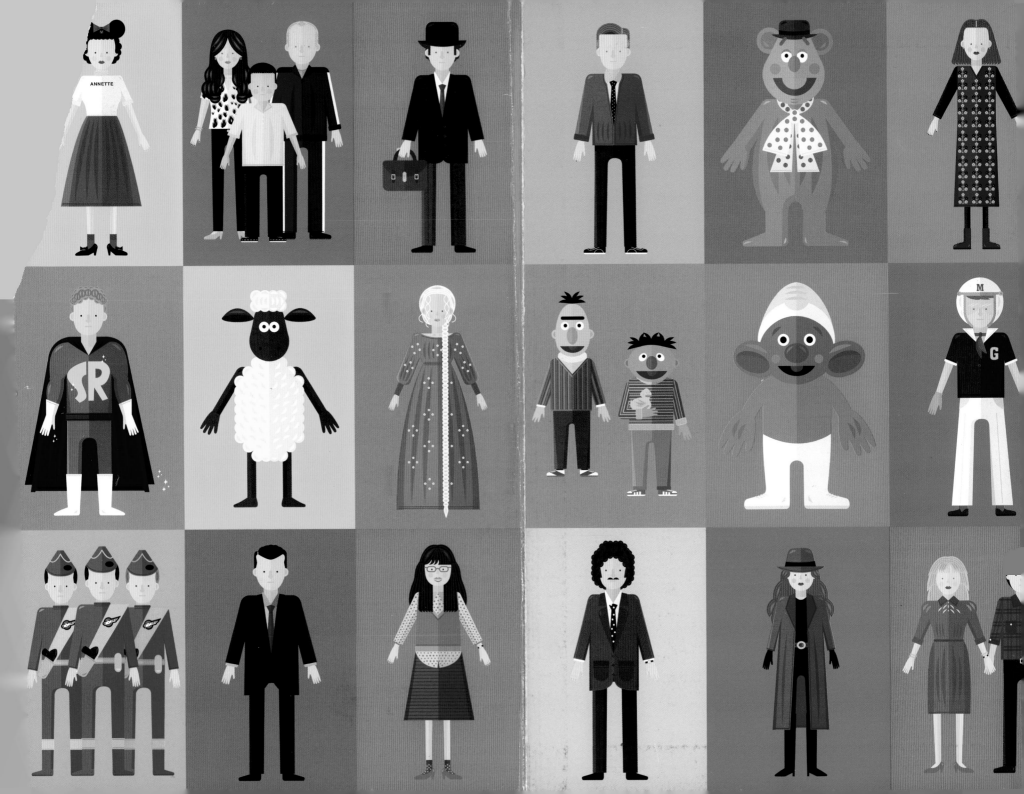